Don Rittner

WATERVLIET
ARSENAL CITY

Copyright 2021 by Don Rittner

All rights reserved. International copyright secured. No part of this book may be reproduced, stored in a retrieval system, or transmitted in any form or by any means electronic, mechanical, photocopying, recording, or otherwise—without the prior written permission of New Netherland Press and Don Rittner, except for the inclusion of brief quotations in an acknowledged review.

ISBN: 978-0-937666-66-1

Dedicated to
Christopher R., Kevin J., Jackson C.
The Rittner Boys

Book design by Don Rittner

New Netherland Press
Schenectady, NY

First Edition

Introduction

This is Volume Three in a series about Watervliet, NY, and its earlier villages of Washington, Port Schuyler, Gibbonsville, and West Troy.

This collection of images deals with the Watervliet Arsenal, an Army-owned and operated manufacturing facility located in the northern part of the city. The arsenal is the oldest, continuously active arsenal in the United States having begun operations during the War of 1812. The arsenal has been making much of the artillery for the United States Army for 209 years. It has been the United States Army's most important center for the development and production of large-caliber weapons but began with the manufacture of small, fixed ammunition and artillery accoutrements, and then became the primary maker of artillery carriages. Since 1887 the arsenal has been the Army's primary producer of large-caliber cannons. In addition it has made gun tubes for cannons, mortars and tanks. It made the country's first 16-inch breech-loading cannon in 1902, and was the Army's only producer of this weapon during the two world wars.

During the Cold War between America and the Soviet Union, it produced the Davey Crockett, or M-28 (light) or M-29 (heavy), a three-person weapon system that was a tactical nuclear recoilless smoothbore gun for firing the M388 nuclear projectile armed with the W54 nuclear warhead that was deployed during the Cold War. It was deployed in May 1961 and aimed at the Soviet Union. Fortunately it never saw combat and was retired in 1971. The Watervliet Historical Society has one on display.

The arsenal was listed on the National Historic Landmark in 1966 and contains a prefabricated cast iron warehouse made in 1859 by Daniel Badger from New York City, one of the first. It served as a museum until 2013 when budget cuts forced its closing and the artifacts were scattered around the country.

Thousands of Watervlieters have worked at the arsenal over the last two centuries. Many old timers and family members remember working at the arsenal and love telling their stories For some it was the centerpiece of their life.

Throughout the book you will become familiar with many of the buildings on the property and what they were used for as well as the importance of the Erie Canal running through the premises. A side cut to the Hudson River allowed the arsenal to place their military products on barges that were used around the world in combat and peacetime. No doubt that many locals will see family and friends who worked there over the years. We thank them for their service.

As always special thanks go to Tom and Marylou Ragosta and the Watervliet Historic Society. The fruits of their research in the text, images and labor are shown in this series of history books on Watervliet.

Don Rittner
December 2021
As always comments and suggestions are welcome at drittner@aol.com

Watervliet Arsenal

The Watervliet Arsenal is America's oldest continuously active Arsenal. It occupies 140 acres on the West side of the Hudson River across from Troy, NY. The entire Arsenal is on the National Register of Historic Sites.

As a result of the War of 1812 with England the United States Army Ordinance Department was given the task of arming troops and providing material support. It was mandated that various arsenals be established around the country. One arsenal was to be located somewhere in upstate New York State so that weapons could be sent either north or west as attacks were expected from the North at Lake Champlain and from the West at Niagara Falls. At the time two small villages were established in what is now Watervliet: Gibbonsville, founded by James Gibbons in 1805, and located between current 8th to 15th Streets, and Washington, founded by the Schuyler family in 1793, and located between current 6th and 8th Streets. This area provided the necessary protection for the possible north and west invasion and also provided the Hudson River as a means of quick shipment of arms to the South.

On June 14, 1813, a deed was signed by James Gibbons and his wife conveying to the United States twelve acres of land for the sum of $2585. This modest purchase initiated the beginning of the Watervliet Arsenal. For the first four years the Arsenal was known as the "Arsenal at Washington and Gibbonsville." By 1817 it was the "Arsenal at Watervliet, NY," as it was located in the Town of Watervliet (now defunct). Thirty more acres of land were purchased from the Gibbons Family in 1828 to the South and in 1833 another forty-five acres was added bringing the total acreage to 82. The US Army gave permission for the Erie Canal to go through the arsenal provided that a fence or wall was built to keep people from easily going into the arsenal and that they could divert and use the water to power machinery. In 1922 the canal was abandoned and in 1941 canal bridges were removed and land leveled. Part of the stone wall is all that remains of the canal.

Lower shops. View from the railroad. 1890. Erie Canal runs through the Arsenal. One of three bridges over the canal in the Arsenal and Building 40 seen in background.

June 10, 1918. Construction of Building 25. Erie canal wall and cast iron warehouse building on the right. Manufacturing sheds beyond Building 25. Note the wagon for moving and dumping dirt with the bottom open and the roller.

Cannon Balls and inverted cannons line the entrance to the arsenal. This main entrance is now closed.

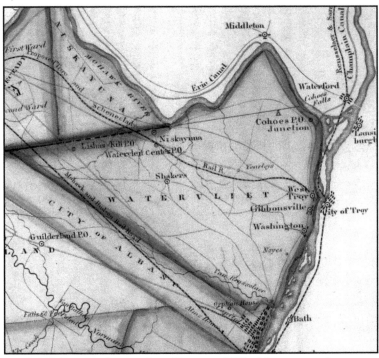

1829. This map shows the villages of Washington and Gibbonsville and West Troy, now the city of Watervliet.

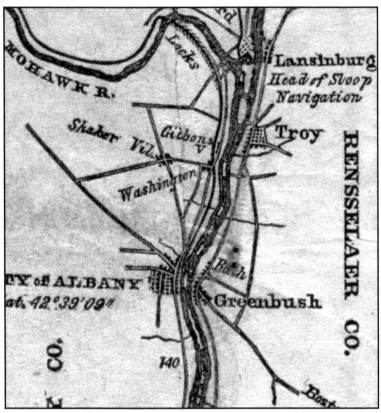

Powell's New Map of the Hudson River. Published around 1830. One of the few maps that show the community named Washington as well as Gibbonsville. West Troy not labeled.

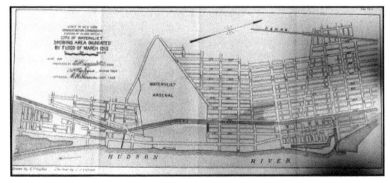

The Flood of March 1913. This map shows the impact of the Great Flood (shaded area) of 1913 on the arsenal.

1900. Steel Bridge. The bridge over the Erie Canal is behind the Administrative Building and the Cannon Community Club (not shown). The cannon carriages and cannon were there for at least 30 years.

Postcard of the first 16 inch gun made at the Watervliet Arsenal. The Master Mechanic and Master Gunmaker who designed and built the 16 inch cannon was Carl Alfred Christiansen. They named the "Big Gun Shop" after him and inducted him into the National Ordnance Hall of Fame.

Capt. Nathaniel R. Potter, Ordnance Officers' Reserve Corps, is assigned to active duty. He will proceed to Watervliet arsenal, Watervliet, N.Y., and report in person to the commanding officer for temporary duty. — The Official Bulletin, 1917.

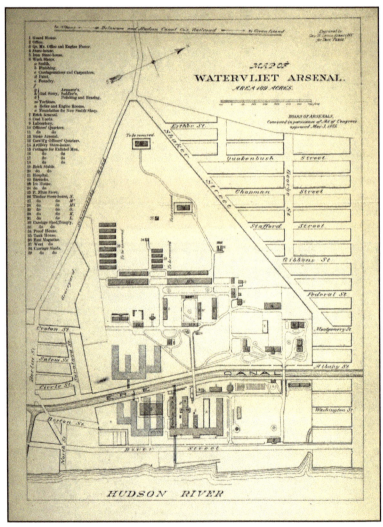

Map of the layout of the Arsenal in 1875 on 108 acres. Notice they had their own streets. Part of the reason it was called Arsenal City.

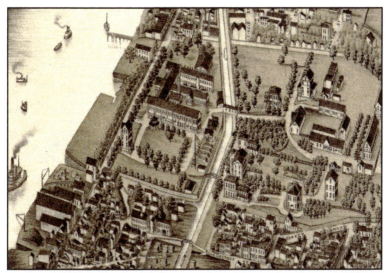

Panorama of part of the Arsenal on an 1888 map. Notice the Erie Canal and bridges over it but now gone except for part of the wall.

Arsenal Cemetery. The Arsenal Cemetery is bounded by the North Arsenal Wall and Route 32 (Broadway) on the East. The deceased were mostly ordinance soldiers who served here in the middle to late 1800s and were buried in the original Gibbonsville Cemetery once located on the South end of Building 110. In 1918 the Arsenal purchased that property from the city of Watervliet and the remaining bodies were removed and relocated to the Albany Rural Cemetery. There are twelve headstones located in the Arsenal Cemetery - 9 that are identified and 3 are unknown.

September 9, 1918. Gibbonsville Cemetery (later named The Watervliet Burial Cemetery). This Cemetery was located on what is now the South end of Building 110. In 1918 the Arsenal bought the property from the City of Watervliet for $1,000 to make way for railroad improvements for the Arsenal shops. Most of the relocated graves were moved to the Albany Rural Cemetery. Below military housing in 1875 and the canal runs through the arsenal.

Many women worked at the Arsenal during WW11 and even in the beginning. More than 3000 woman worked here during WWII making up 30% of the workforce. This is Ms. Frances Kantrowitz drilling the bore of a minor caliber gun in the spring of 1943. Today women workers make up only 11% of the workforce. During the war woman machinists and machine tool operators were as good as their male counterparts.

Watervliet Arsenal inspection Sept 21, 1898. Passed no doubt.

Water outlet from the arsenal. Arsenal building can be seen in the background. Water from the canal was used by the arsenal for its manufacturing processes.

Arsenal Commanders Quarters. Interior view. Tours were once available.

1870. Erie Canal and Bldg. 41. The Administrative Building (1860-1901) is on the left and building 41, the Cannon Community Club, is on the right. Constructed in 1842, this building has been used for an ammunition loading facility, a commissary, an officer's club and an officers mess.

Below is a postcard showing the largest gun in the world made at the Watervliet arsenal.

Large gun ready for shipment. It will be loaded onto a barge on the Hudson River. Circa 1900s

1918. Big Gun Shop. The building is a quarter-mile long and is the arsenal's oldest manufacturing facility.

1918. Troy skyline from Arsenal. Stewart's Stoves in Troy across the river was a large manufacture of cast iron heating stoves. In foreground is the Breech Building built in 1918. Later called Bldg. 25.

Major Stacpole has issues orders for the battalion to assemble again at 1:30 p.m. to escort the visitors to the Watervliet arsenal and other points of interest about the city. — The Argus, September 4, 1899

The bridge over the canal in 1935.

1917. Main Gate entrance to the Watervliet Arsenal. Guard shack in front of octagonal building on right. Building 40 on left and bridge going over the Erie Canal in background. Note the Trolley Tracks on Broadway. Below: Main gate today is no longer open and the inverted cannons are gone. The octagonal gatehouse and trolley tracks are gone too.

1885. Stone Arsenal building in background. Steam operated pumper with three Arsenal Firemen. Behind the pumper is the cannon park were the Arsenal stored cannon and shot after the Civil War. Behind the Erie Canal wall is the three story Arsenal stone building.

Building 125. WWI construction in 1918.

Manufacturing in Building 25 (minor component shop) in 1919.

Activity continues at the gun factory at the Watervliet arsenal. An order has been received from the ordnance department for 1,700 seven-inch howitzer shells and all possible haste will be made in their manufacture. — The Argus, April 21, 1898.

Manufacturing in Building 25 on August 20, 1918.

1870. The Arsenal stored cannon and shot after the Civil War. The Administrative Building (1860-1901) is on the left with the covered bridge over the canal just to the right of the Administrative Building.

Lieut-Col A. R. Buffington, ordnance department, and Anthony Victorin, engineer at Watervliet arsenal, N.Y., have been detailed as members of the board on the army gun factory at Watervliet arsenal, relieving Lieut-Col. F. H. Parker and Capt. J. C. Ayres, ordnance department. First-Lieut. D. A. Howard, ordnance department, has been ordered to duty at the Watervliet arsenal. —The Argus, February 17, 1889.

1870. Cannon storage and covered bridge. The Administrative Building is behind the flagpole and on right is the covered bridge over the canal.

Building 25 constructions site, May 3, 1918

The concrete sidewalk fad in Watervliet is still popular, and a walk on Third avenue extending two blocks south of Fourth street has just been completed. The walks are being laid in all sections of the city, and in many places are replacing the old serviceable flagstones. All these walks have been laid within the past year and followed the one laid in front of the Watervliet arsenal by the United States government, which was the first of the kind to be put down in Watervliet. — The Argus, August 26, 1904.

Building 25 construction on May 25, 1918.

Building 25 constructions site, June 1, 1918

The Watervliet arsenal gun shops are still seeking mechanics, such as skilled machinists, toolmakers, crane operators, carpenters and skilled laborers. It was stated by a workman employed at the plant last night that owing to the scarcity of skilled mechanics, that the government is recalling expert machinists that had been sent to posts to supervise the mounting of newly constructed guns. — The Argus, February 25, 1917.

Building 25 construction on June 10, 1918.

Building 25 construction on June 17, 1918.

Notice that 75 machinists and mechanics are wanted immediately at the Watervliet arsenal. — The Argus, December 18, 1919.

Building 25 construction on June 24, 1918.

Construction on August 20, 1918.

A notice was posted at the Watervliet arsenal gun factory yesterday afternoon notifying the army of employees at the government plant that their vacation starts Friday afternoon, July 3, and will end Friday afternoon. July 24. — The Argus, July 2, 1914.

1918 Building 25 construction completed. Erie Canal in foreground. Part of stone wall separating the canal still on site.

Bridge over the canal, a WPA project in 1935.

Captain J. C. Ayres, of the ordnance department, U. S. A., has reported for duty at the Watervliet arsenal, having been transferred from Benecia arsenal, California. — The Argus, October 28, 1888.

The guardhouse built by the WPA in October, 1936.

View of Building 24 in 1919.

Resolutions favoring the continuation of the cannon and smaller gun making plants at the government arsenal in Watervliet were unanimously adopted at a membership meeting of the Board of Trade held last night.— Cohoes American, March 30, 1920.

Cannon carriages in 1910.

The flagpole and the North bridge.

WWI view in 1918.

The bridge just north of the Arsenal.

Artillery For the Militia. The Ordnance Bureau of the War Department at Washington, under the decision setting apart additional funds for field artillery for the militia, will construct thirty-two guns, the guns to be built at Watervliet arsenal and the carriages at the Rock Island arsenal. — St. Johnsville Enterprise, 1903

View of the lower shops in 1918 from a rooftop.

Workers using belt driven equipment.

The Castleton Merchants defeated the Watervliet Arsenal, 63-59, in a polio benefit game at Maple High Tuesday. The winners, ending the season 23-17, were paced by Bob Leonard with 16 and Ted Dewing with 15. — Times-Union, April 28, 1960.

A dredge and tug boat.

North end of the canal near the Arsenal.

Watervliet Arsenal exit at main gate. Parking lot across Broadway and Troy in background. Parking lot now part of I-787.

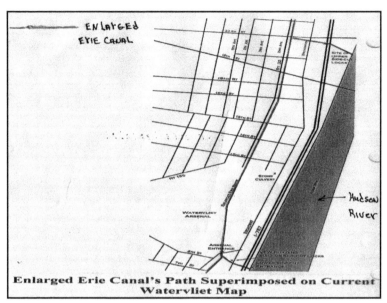

Erie Canal through Arsenal Circa 1860.

Woman standing on electric shop truck, Watervliet Arsenal, Watervliet, NY, during World War I.

Stockpile of cannonballs at the Watervliet Arsenal.

It is estimated that the Watervliet Arsenal at Watervliet, N. Y., can turn out 560 guns in a year, running twenty-four hours a day — Olean NY Evening Times, February, 29, 1913

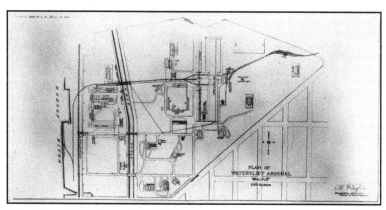

The Watervliet Arsenal in 1894.

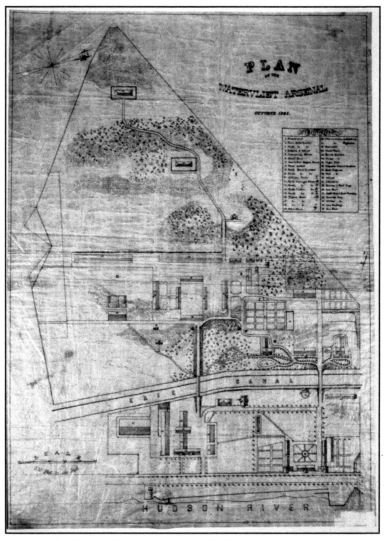

Map of the Watervliet Arsenal in 1863. Source LOC.

A cannon manufactured at Watervliet arsenal for Civil War use but rejected because of flaws will be taken from the Perry High school grounds, where it has stood for more than 50 years for conversion to the war effort. — Poughkeepsie Eagle News, April 23, 1942.

Watervliet Arsenal. No date, probably late 19th century. Source LOC.

Canal boats line up near the Arsenal. West Troy was a main starting point for immigration to the West. NY Harbor, as a result of the Erie, surpassed all others in traffic along the Eastern Seaboard. Emigrants travelled up the Hudson and entered the canal at West Troy on their way to the West.

Watervliet Arsenal, Cast-Iron Storehouse, Westervelt Avenue & Gibson Street. Daniel Badger from NYC built this all cast iron building. Badger and James Bogardus are the fathers of cast iron for architecture. In 1842 Badger erected the first cast iron storefront ever in America in Boston. Until recently used as an excellent military museum, "Museum of the Big Guns," but closed in 2013 as one person put it by "Gov't budget-slashing terrorists." Built in 1859. Bldg. No. 38.

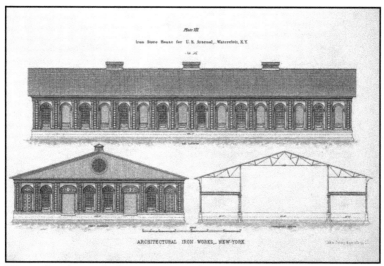

Watervliet Arsenal, Cast-Iron Storehouse. Drawings and descriptions in Badger's catalog of 1865. Plate XII. Front and end elevation and section of Iron Store House, erected for the U. S. Government at Watervliet Arsenal, West Troy, NY. This building is entirely of iron above the foundation. Plate XIII. Section and elevation of Pier and Arch, and section of Cornice and Arch, Iron Store House, Watervliet Arsenal.

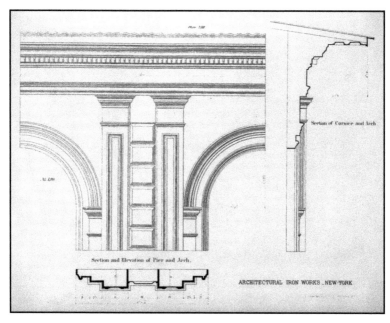

Watervliet Arsenal. 1940. US Army armaments. Gun Shell Tank.

Watervliet Arsenal employed nearly 2000 workers during the Civil War.

Early 1900s. Rifling Big Guns.

Building 145 & 146. Large Caliber Gun Tube Bldg. Gillespie Rd south of Parker Rd. Built 1942-43.

The Watervliet Arsenal on November 20, 1917, was instructed to do the machining of forgings so as to turn out 250 gun bodies for the 240 - millimeter howitzers, and three months later this order was doubled. — 1919.

Arsenal workers 1893-95.

The Arsenal had its own fire department.

The Cold War Davy Crockett was produced in two variants: the "light" M28 120 mm recoilless rifle and the "heavy" M29 155 mm recoilless rifle. The M28 had a range of approximately 1.25 miles (2 kilometers), while the larger M29 could launch a projectile out to 2.5 miles (4 kilometers). Both variants fired the 76-pound M388 atomic projectile, which had a diameter of eleven inches and a length of thirty-one inches.

Erie Canal and Buildings 38, 40 and 41. 1905. Rear barge is named Adlai Stevenson (a Democrat). Two barges traveling through the Erie Canal at the Watervliet Arsenal. Both are tied together and are being towed by two mules on the right. Both barges have portable bridges shown on top for bringing the mules on and off the barge. Power to run the machines in the manufacturing buildings was obtained by sluicing water from the canal into turbines located in the basement and then dumping the water into the Hudson. Below. Labor poster during WWII honoring workers.

NEW FENCE — New sidewalks and fencing along Broadway were completed under WPA in 1936

1936. New sidewalks and fence on Broadway opposite the main gate of Arsenal. The rest of Watervliet followed.

First 16 inch gun made in 1895.

World War 1 Poster

Panorama of the Arsenal in 1888.

For boring and turning lathes, rifling machine, and eighty-ton traveling-crane fully equipped for the manufacture of twelve-inch guns, at Watervliet Arsenal, New York, three hundred and twenty thousand dollars. —1890.

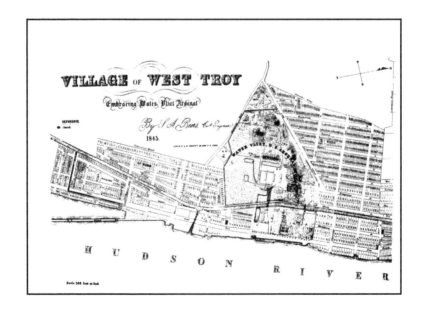

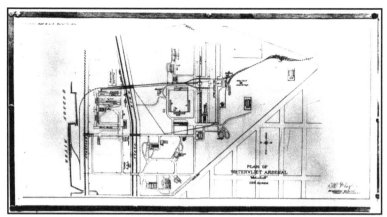
Plan of the Arsenal in 1834.

Various buildings at the arsenal. Bird's eye view. N.D.

An aerial view of the arsenal complex of buildings, looking east into Troy.

The Benet Lab. See the trolley tracks going down Broadway. Named for General Stephen Vincent Benet who was the 8th Chief of Ordnance for the US Army Ordnance Corps. His grandson was the writer Pulitzer Prize winner Stephen Vincent Benet.

Canal boats going through the arsenal with its high retaining wall.

For railroad sidings, switches, and weighing scale at the army gun factory, Watervliet arsenal, New York, two thousand eight hundred dollars. For one hundred and fifty horse- power steam-engine and shafting for machine-shop at the army gun factory, Watervliet arsenal, New York. Three thousand five hundred dollars — 1890

Canal near the Arsenal. Bridge and Stone Mansion visible.

A view of the canal walls through the arsenal. Parts visible today.

For machinery to complete the full capacity of present gun factory building at Watervliet Arsenal, West Troy, New York, one hundred and sixty-five thousand dollars. For erection and completion of a fire-proof brick office building for the army gunfactory, Watervliet Arsenal, New York, twenty three thousand dollars. — 1890.

Engraving of loading shipment at the arsenal at West Troy.

Top and Bottom. Cannons on a barge *The Rockland Lake Trap* on the Hudson. The city of Troy across the river showing Ludlow Steel and Stewart Stove Company. Their products and arsenal products left on the Watervliet sidecuts for NYC.

Top & Bottom. Watervliet Arsenal, Building No. 10, Buffington Street west of Dalliba Avenue. Since its construction as the arsenal HQs in 1894, the building has served a central role in Watervliet's history. Its original construction and subsequent additions reflect various periods of growth at the arsenal. LOC photo and info.

Top & Bottom. Watervliet Arsenal, Building No. 4, Mordecai Drive, west of Mettler Road, This building is an intact integral element of the officers' family housing area developed at the North side of the arsenal during the 19th century to house the installation's highest ranking officers. Built in 1867. LOC photo and info.

Top & Bottom. Watervliet Arsenal, Building No. 2, Bricker Lane, south of Stewart Road. Erected in 1889, One of two similar quarters built to house an increased officer staff necessitated by establishment of the Army's gun factory at Watervliet. Located in the housing area developed at the North side of the arsenal in the 19th century, it's a good example of a Queen Anne style residence. Among the building's residents were the family of Colonel James Walker Benet. LOC photo and info.

Top & Bottom. Watervliet Arsenal, Building No. 6, Mettler Road, north of Mordecai Drive. The building is an intact and integral element of the quarters area developed at the North end of the arsenal during the 19th century to house the installation's high ranking officers. Designed by the arsenal's commander nearly a decade before it was constructed, the building reflects the appearance of the nearby commandant's quarters. Built in 1848. LOC photo and info.

Top & Bottom. Watervliet Arsenal, Building No. 24, Arnold Lane, south of Westervelt Avenue. The building is an excellent and largely intact example of early permanent construction at the arsenal. As the only example of enlisted troop housing surviving on its original site, the building also contributes to an understanding of the arsenal's overall history. Built in 1843. LOC photo and info.

Dowling & Campbell have received the contract for furnishing the Iron beams, roof trusses, and iron stairways for the new office building now in process of erection on the Watervliet arsenal grounds. — The Evening Standard, August, 14, 1894.

Top & Bottom. Watervliet Arsenal, Building No. 3, Mordecai Drive south of Stewart Road. Erected in 1889, this building is one of two similar quarters built to house an increased officer staff necessitated by establishment of the Army's gun factory at Watervliet. Located in the housing area developed at the North side of the arsenal in the 19th century, it is a good example of a Queen Anne style residence. LOC photo and info.

Top & Bottom. Watervliet Arsenal, Building No. 12, Farley Drive, SE of Bricker Lane. The building is an intact example of early 20th century greenhouse construction. It is a vestige of the time when the Army ornamented its installations with formal gardens and is probably one of the few remaining Army-owned greenhouse structures. LOC photo and info. The city now owns this greenhouse for public display someday.

Top & Bottom. Watervliet Arsenal, Building No. 40, Broadway between Dalliba & Watervliet Avenues. Benet Research & Engineering Laboratory. As Watervliet's center of manufacture between about 1840 and 1886, the building served an important role in the arsenal's history. Built in 1840. It is the US Army's design authority for large caliber armaments and safe life considerations. Benét is also responsible for the full life-cycle of mortars, tank guns, and artillery cannon for howitzers; provides tank turret support for ABRAMS and Crew Cooling for ABRAMS, Bradley and LAV combat vehicles; and provides support to the Army's industrial base at the Watervliet Arsenal. LOC photo and info.

Top & Bottom. Big Gun Shop. Watervliet Arsenal, Building No. 110, Hagner Road between Schull & Whittemore Roads. 1888-1892. Additions 1917-1941. The building is significant for its historic role as America's center for large caliber weapons manufacture since the late nineteenth century and because of its distinction as a work of nineteenth-century industrial design. Built in 1891. LOC photo and info. 1245 feet in length, 125 feet wide except where widened to 1-story. Inside is a high bridge crane. Originally the Sea Coast Gun Shop.

Top & Bottom. Watervliet Arsenal, Building No. 1, Mettler Road between Dalliba Avenue & Bricker Lane. The building has served as the commandant's quarters (Quarters One) since its construction in 1841. It is the earliest of five residences built at the North end of the arsenal during the 19th century to house the installation's highest ranking officers. James Walker Benet of Kentucky was Chief of Ordnance at the arsenal from 1904-05 and 1919-21. It has been reported that the poet and writer Stephen Vincent Benet was the son of James Walker Benet and lived there but newer research shows that it may be a different person and not related. LOC photo and info.

Watervliet Arsenal, Building 105, South Broadway, on Hudson River. Built in 1836 part and 1918. LOC photo and info.

Watervliet Arsenal, Building No. 135, Gillespie Road, south of Parker Road. The building is a major component of manufacturing facilities constructed at Watervliet Arsenal during World War II and is a building in which advanced technology was employed in the manufacture of large caliber guns. Built in 1942-43. LOC photo and info.

Watervliet Arsenal, Building No. 22, Westervelt Avenue & Buffington Street. One of two similar structures apparently built in 1839 as carriage storehouses, this building represents one of the few remaining vestiges of carriage making and storage, an important element of nineteenth-century manufacture at the arsenal. LOC photo and info.

Watervliet Arsenal, Building 14, South Broadway, on Hudson River. Built 1845. Two story brick shed for lumber storage, later converted in 1887 to a field and siege gun shop. LOC photo and info.

Watervliet Arsenal, Building No. 129, Worth Road near Baker Road. The building is a highly intact example of early ammunition magazine design and contributes to an understanding of the arsenal's early manufacturing and storage activities. It was modeled after the "East Magazine," the arsenal's oldest standing structure. Date 1849. LOC photo and info.

Watervliet Arsenal, Building No. 15, Buffington Street between Symington Street & Dalliba Avenue. One of two similar structures apparently built in 1839 as carriage storehouses, this building represents one of the few remaining vestiges of carriage making and storage, an important element of nineteenth-century manufacture at the arsenal. Previously lumber warehouse. Built 1839. LOC photo and info.

Watervliet Arsenal, Building 30, South Broadway, on Hudson River. Carpenter shop. Built 1918. LOC photo and info.

Watervliet Arsenal is located within the city limits of Watervliet, N. Y. Its main function is the manufacture of both light and heavy guns, and accessories. The site was acquired in 1813, and comprises 144 acres. The value of its lands, buildings and equipment is $12,029,000. During the World War employees numbered 3,300 and production in 1918 was 578 completed guns, ranging from 1.457 - inch to 16 - inch. There were relined or modified 161 guns, ranging from 6 to 16 - inch types — 1922

Watervliet Arsenal, Building 116, South Broadway, on Hudson River. Oil storage building. Built 1907. LOC photo and info.

Watervliet Arsenal, Building No. 41, Gibson Street & Dalliba Street. The building represents early ammunition manufacturing and handling activity at the arsenal and was an adjunct facility to the Broadway shops. Together the laboratory and shops comprised Watervliet's manufacturing center from 1840 until the mid-1880s when the arsenal was designated the Army's gun factor. Built 1840. LOC photo and info.

Watervliet Arsenal, Building No. 17, Arnold Lane, south of Dalliba Avenue. Originally constructed in 1830 as a storehouse for nitre, this building is one of the oldest and most highly intact structures at the arsenal. LOC photo and info.

Watervliet Arsenal, Building 28, South Broadway, on Hudson River. Storage shed. Built 1914. LOC photo and info.

Watervliet Arsenal, Building 108, South Broadway, on Hudson River. Maintenance office, Built 1890. LOC photo and info.

Watervliet Arsenal, Building 104, South Broadway, on Hudson River. Steel Stock Storage Building. Built 1918. LOC photo and info.

Watervliet Arsenal, Building 103, South Broadway, on Hudson River. Latrine Building. Built 1917. LOC photo and info.

Watervliet Arsenal, Building 101, South Broadway, on Hudson River. Oil Storage Building. Built 1919. LOC photo and info.

Watervliet Arsenal, Building 33, South Broadway, on Hudson River. Storage Shed (Building Material). Built 1944. LOC photo and info.

Watervliet Arsenal, Building 27, South Broadway, on Hudson River. Storage Shed (lumber). Built 1940. LOC photo and info.

Watervliet Arsenal, Building 26, South Broadway, on Hudson River. Storage Shed (Building material). Built 1942. LOC photo and info.

Watervliet Arsenal, Building 32, South Broadway, on Hudson River. Gate House, NW corner. Built 1920. LOC photo and info.

A handsome white marble foundation is being erected at the Watervliet Arsenal. — The Argus, May 3, 1900.

Watervliet Arsenal, Building 112, South Broadway, on Hudson River. Proof Range. Built 1918. LOC photo and info.

Watervliet Arsenal, Building 106, South Broadway, on Hudson River. LOC photo and info.

Watervliet Arsenal, Building No. 119, Munroe Street between Hagner & Worth Roads. Laboratory and command operating center. Built 1828. LOC photo and info.

Watervliet Arsenal, Building 34, South Broadway, on Hudson River. Storage building (paint). Built 1949, SE corner. LOC photo and info.

Watervliet Arsenal, Building 31, South Broadway, on Hudson River. Condensate Return Pump House. Built 1918. SW corner. LOC photo and info.

Heavy hardware. Building the slide seats for medium-caliber guns being produced for national defense in an eastern arsenal. Palmer, Alfred T., photographer. 1942. LOC photo and info.

The new rifled gun, the first to be made at the Watervliet gun foundry, has passed safely through the ordeals of the shrinking pit and the boring and rifling lathes, and now rests flawless and in all the majesty of its fifteen tons of cold steel upon a temporary bed, in the makeshift shop, where it has been, for months past, slowly taking form, Its grim muzzle pointing toward Albany. — The Argus, August 11, 1889.

Oversized shootin' iron. Machining a breech block seat for a mighty gun being rushed for completion in an eastern arsenal. Palmer, Alfred T., photographer. 1942. LOC photo and info.

Activity at Uncle Sam's big gun plant at the Watervliet arsenal, where the mammoth implements of war for coast defense are manufactured, continues without abatement. For the second time since the close of the civil war, the small gun shop was in operation yesterday, when a large force of men labored assiduously, bringing the guns to a nearer state of completion. The building known as the "Canteen," at the arsenal, is being converted into a laboratory, where metallic cartridges will be manufactured. — The Argus, April 25, 1898.

Putting the parts together. Fitting the breech ring seat on one of the medium caliber guns rolling from a large eastern arsenal working full speed for victory. Palmer, Alfred T., photographer. 1942. LOC photo and info.

Polishing up a big one. Worker in a large eastern arsenal smoothing off one of the many big guns Uncle Sam needs for the war against the Axis. Palmer, Alfred T., photographer. 1942. LOC photo and info.

The man behind the gun. Worker in an eastern arsenal finishing up the breech end of a tube of a medium-caliber gun for the war program. Palmer, Alfred T., photographer. 1942. LOC photo and info.

Equipment for a grim game. Medium-caliber guns roll in a growing stream from a large eastern arsenal as the war program reaches full schedule. Palmer, Alfred T., photographer. 1942. LOC photo and info.

The funeral of James A. Shaughnessy, the victim of Thursday's explosion at the Watervliet arsenal, will be held tomorrow afternoon at 2 o'clock from his late home on Fourth avenue, Watervliet, and afterwards from St. Patrick's church. — The Argus, November 18, 1899.

Making accuracy certain. Rifling grooves to speed shells on their way with accuracy are cut in a medium-caliber gun in a large eastern arsenal. Palmer, Alfred T., photographer. 1942. LOC photo and info.

Rounding out the job. Worker in an eastern arsenal machines the breech end of a major caliber gun nearing completion in the nation's huge war production program. Palmer, Alfred T., photographer. 1942. LOC photo and info.

Covering the compass. Partially-completed big guns point north, east, south and west toward our borders as they await finishing operations in a large eastern arsenal. Palmer, Alfred T., photographer. 1942. LOC photo and info.

Crozier 10 - inch wire gun — The manufacture of this gun was under taken under the provisions of the act of September 22, 1888, and Watervliet Arsenal was selected as the place of manufacture. — Report of the Chief of Ordnance to the Secretary of War, 1893.

Going down! Partially assembled, a big gun is lowered into the shrinkage pit of an eastern arsenal, where the cannon is nearing completion for the war program. Palmer, Alfred T., photographer. 1942. LOC photo and info.

February 1886. A bill was passed to provide for the establishment of a gun foundry at Watervliet Arsenal, West Troy, N. Y., for finishing and assembling guns adapted to modern warfare, and for the manufacture of gun carriages and ordnance equipments, and authorizes the Secretary of war to make contracts with responsible steel manufacturers for materials for heavy ordinance adapted to modern warfare, and appropriates $8,000,000.

Giving defense a lift. A mighty crane installs one of the big machines in a large eastern arsenal. The apparatus going in is a major capacity cylindrical grinder. Palmer, Alfred T., photographer. 1942. LOC photo and info.

Biggest Gun in the World. The 16-inch gun, the biggest in the world, which is being built at the Watervliet arsenal, will be sent to the proving grounds at Sandy Hook next fall. The gun will be finished by July. — The Argus, March 12, 1901.

Taking care of the kick-back. Recoil rails are assembled for a medium caliber gun rushed for the war production program in an eastern arsenal. Palmer, Alfred T., photographer. 1942. LOC photo and info.

Answering the call. Dozens of partially-machined tubes for medium caliber guns await finishing processes in an eastern arsenal. Every day finds Uncle Sam's defensive armament stronger. Palmer, Alfred T., photographer. 1942. LOC photo and info.

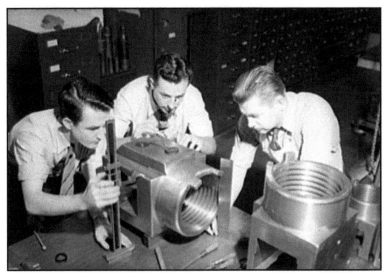

Check and triple check. Final inspection of breach rings for medium caliber guns in an eastern arsenal. Greatest accuracy marks production in the war program. Palmer, Alfred T., photographer. 1942. LOC photo and info.

Accuracy comes first. Experienced inspectors check clip hoops for the ultimate in accuracy. The operation is part of the rush of defense orders in an eastern arsenal. Palmer, Alfred T., photographer. 1942. LOC photo and info.

Where there's smoke. A worker in an eastern arsenal turns the thread surface on a medium-caliber gun. Note the wisp of smoke rising from the point where the thread is being cut. Palmer, Alfred T., photographer. 1942. LOC photo and info.

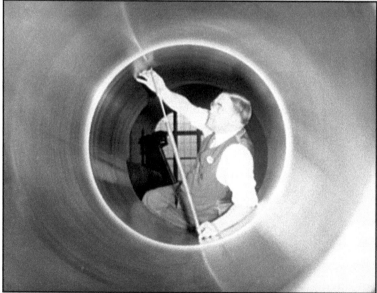

A smoothy enlists. Polished interior surface of a big gun for Uncle Sam's war program. The bore diameter of hoop is measured in the large eastern arsenal where the work is carried on. Palmer, Alfred T., photographer. 1942. LOC photo and info.

Voices for a mighty argument. A long line of big guns being rushed toward completion under the war production program. Guns shown here are being turned out in the major caliber shop of a large eastern arsenal. Palmer, Alfred T., photographer. 1942. LOC photo and info.

Business district. Bench workers finishing a breech housing for a medium caliber gun in a large eastern arsenal. This is a section of the business part of one of the guns being turned out for the war production program. Palmer, Alfred T., photographer. 1942. LOC photo and info.

On the "assembly" line. Scores of parts go into Uncle Sam's big guns. Worker at a large eastern arsenal inspects some of the mechanism parts for medium-caliber guns. The utmost accuracy is required to ensure efficient performance. LOC photo and info.

Big throat, big voice. Boring operations are finished on a major-caliber gun at an eastern arsenal. This big boy will soon be ready to speak with authority for total warfare. Palmer, Alfred T., photographer. 1942. LOC photo and info.

Every knock a boost. A little careful hammer work pushes a big gun along toward completion in an eastern arsenal. The man shown is stamping the location line on a medium-caliber gun. Palmer, Alfred T., photographer. 1942. LOC photo and info.

Mary Corbett, 7 years old, who was accidentally shot by a guard at the Watervliet arsenal Saturday afternoon is on the road to recover. — The Argus, July 27, 1914.

Another batch coming up. Parts for dozens of small guns are checked for accuracy in an eastern arsenal. These are breach rings that will soon be fitted into cannons for the war program. Palmer, Alfred T., photographer. 1942. LOC photo and info.

At the office at the Watervliet arsenal yesterday afternoon it was announced that Lieut. Col. Charles A. Walker, stationed at present at the Sandy Hook testing grounds, will come to the Watervliet arsenal, Saturday, June 20, to succeed the late Liet. Col. Legrand B. Curtis. — The Argus, June 4, 1914.

Rolling em' out. Tubes and liners for medium caliber guns are prepared for finishing operations in an eastern arsenal. The cannons are being rushed for the war program. "All out for defense." Palmer, Alfred T., photographer. 1942. LOC photo and info.

For the ramparts. A series of medium caliber guns nears completion in an eastern arsenal. Men shown are engaged in the exterior inspection of liners on guns for the war production program. Palmer, Alfred T., photographer. 1942. LOC photo and info.

There will be a meeting this afternoon at 4 o'clock of the committee on playgrounds and recreation facilities. Rev Dr. George Dugan is chairman of the committee. The committee will also cooperate with the government officials in providing playground and recreation facilities for the new works at the Watervliet arsenal and their families — The Argus, April 23, 1919.

No margin for error here. Micrometer readings are taken to make sure that every part fits perfectly in the guns being manufactured for war purposes. This worker is inspecting a breech ring for medium-caliber guns in a large eastern arsenal. Palmer, Alfred T., photographer. 1942. LOC photo and info.

Big gun made at the arsenal ready for shipping.

Within a few days orders will be issued from the war department relieving Lieut.-Col. Charles Shaler from his duty as commandant of the Watervliet arsenal. His successor at that position has not yet been selected. —The Argus, April 21, 1903.

Loading a cannon onto barge on the Hudson probably at the lower side cut. Troy is across the river.

"As the oldest continuously active arsenal in the United States, Watervliet Arsenal has provided much needed ordnance and materiel in all but one of America's conflicts—the Revolutionary War." Col. Earl B. Schonberg Jr., 61st commander. July 14, 2021

The one hundred and fifty ton gun scale of the Watervliet Arsenal. Scientific American article on May 26, 1894.

A portion of the arsenal from the 1877 Bailey and Hazen map. Below is a 1873 map.

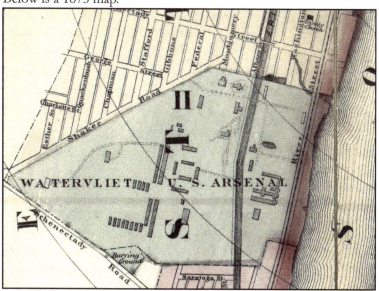

THE ARGUS: SUNDAY MORNING, APRIL 24, 1898.

FIGHT FOR THE ARSENAL.

How Gen. Tracey Secured the Appropriation for Watervliet.

To a great extent, the credit for having this country on a good war basis in so short a time is due to General Charles Tracey, who served from the Albany district in Congress for eight years. When General Tracey was a member of the Fiftieth Congress, and made his greatest fight for the establishment of a gun factory at Watervliet, the probability of a war existed in no man's mind. General Tracey believed in Washington's well known maxim, "In time of peace prepare for war," and he energetically worked to have a gun factory established at Watervliet, where great guns and projectiles might be manufactured for the army.

He was successful, and large appropriations were made. Big guns and projectiles have been turned out in large numbers. General Traceys' foresight has redounded to the best possible interest of the government.

At Watervliet arsenal, before General Tracey began his labors, harness was made, 3 2-10-inch guns were manufactured, and some small projectiles. In 1885 there had been a board appointed to inquire into the subject and advisability of building an army gun factory. The board examined various arsenals, including Watervliet, and merely reported that "Watervliet arsenal was well situated." When General Tracey became congressman he immediately commenced his work. He saw General Benet, chief of ordnance, and told him that he wished to introduce a bill establishing a gun factory at Watervliet. He co-operated with General Benet and a bill was drafted, which General Tracey introduced. It was for an appropriation of $1,000,000. The bill was promptly referred to the committee on military affairs and reported favorably. The House appropriation committee that was to have handled the bill was not in favor of the bill. In the Senate, after the military appropriation bill had passed the House, Chairman Hawley, of the Senate committee, put the million-dollar appropriation for the Watervliet gun factory as a rider on the military appropriation bill. When the appropriation bill came back to the House, General Tracey tried to have it passed with his amendment, but the appropriation committee fought it. It received one favorable vote, but on the second ballot it seemed to be doomed. In the committee of the whole bill was being considered, and General Tracey made the point of order that there was no quorum present. Congressmen hastened to him and prevailed on him to withdraw the point and to have the matter adjusted in conference. Believing that members of the military committee would be appointed on the conference committee, the point was withdrawn, but the speaker appointed two members from the appropriation committee and only one from the military committee. A deadlock resulted. The Senate wouldn't give way, so the appropriation committee brought in a fortification bill for $730,000 for Watervliet.

The bill was sent to the Senate and there was cut to $500,000. Chairman Plumb was hastily consulted by Gen. Tracey, and the senator finally said in answer to General Tracey's arguments that if the House would hold out the Senate would yield. So the $730,000 appropriation was secured and the north wing was built. The following year $100,000 was secured for the south wing. Many other appropriations were secured in the fortification bills that were passed in subsequent years, these being for big guns, projectiles, etc.

The Watervliet arsenal is now, thanks to Congressman Tracey's efforts, the greatest and finest in the world, even better than the celebrated Krupps factory in Germany. Had there been a less influential man in Congress, or a man who was less energetic, Watervliet gun factory would never have been in evidence, and the country might have been in worse shape for big coast defense guns, projectiles, etc., than it is to-day to face the great emergency whish has so suddenly arisen.

CAPTAIN FRANK R. PALMER,
Company A.

This arsenal reservation contains 109 acres; the river front is 1,600 feet long, 800 feet of which is finished as a stone wharf where vessels as large as any navigating the upper Hudson can unload. From the river it extends westward with a width of 1,700 feet to the Erie canal, (passing through about 600 feet from the river) and thence in triangular shape to a point about 1,000 feet from the canal and within 200 feet of the track of the Delaware and Hudson Co.'s railroad, which could there be connected by rail at small expense with all the arsenal shops and stores. — P. V. Hagner, Colonel of Ordnance, Commanding. March 26, 1878.

THE MAN WITHIN THE GUN.

Here is the 16-inch gun which has just been completed at the Watervliet arsenal. This view shows the muzzle, with a man in it whose weight is 165 pounds. The gun is immense, when one considers the quality of the metal contained in it, which is, of course, the best that science and skill can produce at the present time. It is built up of nine pieces of steel forgings, the first piece being the tube, all in one piece, 48 feet long. The whole length of the finished gun is 49 feet, the diameter at breech end is 5½ feet, and at muzzle 2 feet 4 inches. Its weight is 130 tons, and it is rifled with 96 grooves. The breech-loading mechanism is operated by the one movement of turning a crank. Twenty turns of the crank swings the breech block out ready for the firing, which is done by pulling a lanyard after the primer has been placed in position and connected with electric contact. The firing mechanism is connected so as to make it impossible to explode the primer before the breech block is properly closed and locked.

Oregon State Misc Newspaper - 1902, featuring the big 16-inch gun. Below is a photograph of the barrel without the man inside.

Watervliet Arsenal celebrated 208 years of service and support to America's military with a cake-cutting ceremony lead by the arsenal's 61st commander Col. Earl B. Schonberg, Jr. July 14, 2021.

Watervliet Arsenal will install new machines in the historic 'Big Gun Shop' to increase cannon production capacity.
— September 9, 2019

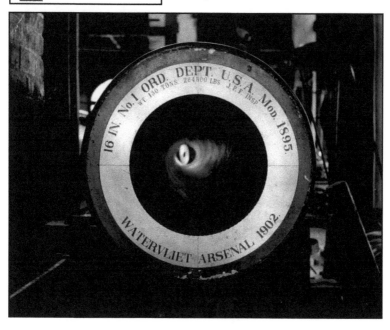

Watervliet Arsenal Partial Commanders List

Assumed	Relieved	Rank	Name	Cullum	Notes
1851	1857	Maj.	Symington, John	126	
1857	1861	Maj.	Mordecai, Alfred	326	
1861-05-14	1863-12-17	Maj.	Thornton, William A.	403	Promoted Lt.-Colonel Mar. 3, 1863
1861-05	1861-07	'1st Lt.	Strong, George C.	1764	Temporary commander, apparently during the absence of the preceding.
1863-12-25	1866-08-12	Lt. Col.	Hagner, Peter V.	866	
1880-12-03	1881-09-29	Maj.	Buffington, Adelbert R.	1894	Promoted Lt.-Colonel June 1, 1881.
1881-11-02	1886-05-24	Lt. Col.	Mordecai, Alfred	1941	
1886-06-05		Lt. Col.	Whittemore, James M.	1854	Cullum's *Register* gives no indication of when he relinquished command. He was promoted Colonel Jan. 3, 1887.
1889-11-21	1892-12-12	Lt. Col.	Parker, Francis H.	1952	
1893	1898	Maj.	Arnold, Isaac	1979	Promoted Lt.-Colonel Feb. 22, 1897.
1898-02-23	1899-05-05	-Col.	Mordecai, Alfred	1941	
1899-05-26	1903-02-18	-Col.	Farley, Joseph P.	1953	
1905-04	1907-10-31	Maj.	MacNutt, Ira	2329	Promoted Lt.-Colonel June 25, 1906.
1908-01	1918-02-15	Lt. Col.	Gibson, William Wesley	2765	Promoted Colonel Sep. 2, 1912.
1919-03-10	1921-07-16	Lt. Col.	Bénét, J. Walker	2860	
1929-09-29	1932-02-28	-Col.	Schull, Herman W.	3886	
1945-04-01	1946-04-30	-Col.	Partridge, Clarence E.	4766	

Dates are formatted in yyyy-mm-dd to sort correctly.

The Cullum Number is the graduation order from the United States Military Academy by year and class rank and links to a page for the officer on the website version of the Cullum Register. Listings without a Cullum Number indicate that the person was not a graduate of the United States Military Academy.

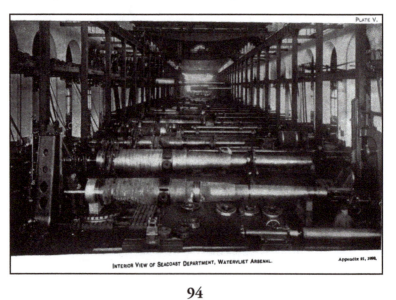

PLATE V.

INTERIOR VIEW OF SEACOAST DEPARTMENT, WATERVLIET ARSENAL.

Appendix 21, 1898.

Interior of arsenal building. No date or location.

In 1962 this 16-inch gun was on a lathe ready to be machined.

A visit from President Roosevelt in October 1940.

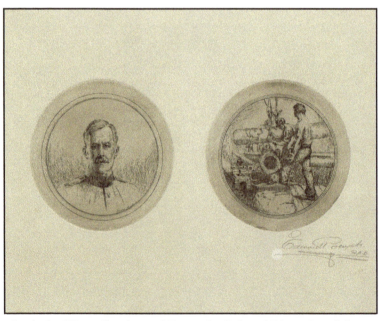
Study for Watervliet Arsenal Poster by Edward Pierre Buyck in 1918. Smithsonian Institution archives.

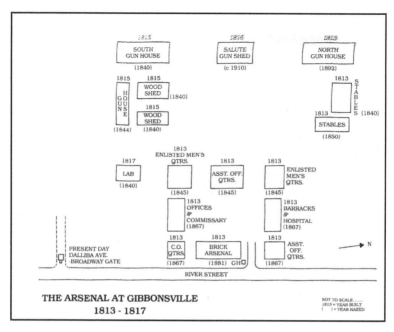

M1895 16-inch gun in chain slings at dock loading for Sandy Hook.

Interested in Reading More about the History of the Arsenal? Here are some links to several Internet sources that you can download or read online.

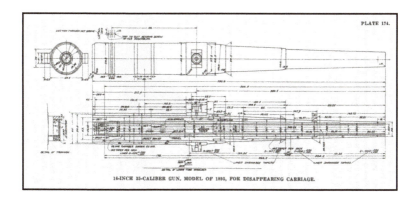

16-INCH 35-CALIBER GUN, MODEL OF 1895, FOR DISAPPEARING CARRIAGE.

Go to Google Books and type in these titles:

The Watervliet Arsenal. Letter address to Hon. Martin I. Townsend, from General P. V. Hagner, Commandant at Arsenal, 1879. 6 pp.

The Watervliet Arsenal: A Chronology of the Nation's Oldest Arsenal. James V. Murray and John Swantek, 1993. Download this book at https://archive.org/details/watervlietarsena00wash

Biographical Register of the Offices and Graduates of the U.S. Military Academy from 1802 to 1867. George Washington Cullum. Applewood Books, 1879.

Or you can join the official Watervliet Arsenal Facebook page at:

https://www.facebook.com/WatervlietArsenal

Team Work by Edward Pierre Buyck. n.d. Smithsonian Institution archives.

The history of Watervliet was written up in the Bicentennial History of Albany by Howell and Tenney and titled *"History of the County of Albany, N.Y., From 1609 to 1886."* It was published by W.W. Munsell & Co publishers in New York.

Both the histoty of West Troy and the Town of Watervliet are reproduced here. Of course the 20th century and current history of Watervliet is being collected by the wonderful volunteers of the Watervliet Historical Society.

Most of the research in this book was supplied by the Watervliet Historical Society.

HISTORY OF THE VILLAGE OF WEST TROY.

By V. J. OOTHOUT.

THE village of West Troy is located on the east bank of the Hudson River, and directly opposite to the city of Troy, Rensselaer County.

This village and the village of Green Island are within and comprise a part of the town of Watervliet, Albany County, and are the only incorporated villages within the town. The northern portion of the village of West Troy is located on the Mohawk River, as the most southern of the many mouths, or "sprouts," of this river empties into the Hudson River at this point, and in so doing forms the island called Green Island.

The land upon which these villages are located is a part of the land owned by Kiliaen Van Rensselaer, of the manor of Rensselaerwick.

The village of West Troy was incorporated as a village by an act of legislature, passed April 30, 1836, and by this act it took within its corporate limits what had theretofore been known as the villages of Port Schuyler, Gibbonsville and West Troy.

None of these villages, except Gibbonsville, had ever been incorporated. Port Schuyler was that part of the present village which lies south of the lands now owned and used by the United States as an arsenal, and was originally a part of the farm of John Schuyler and Peter Schuyler, and was purchased in 1827 of the said Schuylers, by Willard Earl, Jabes Burrows, Abijab Wheeler, David Wheeler, Enoch Burrows, Gilbert C. Bedell and Jonathan Hart. These purchasers were called and known as the Port Schuyler Company. After the purchase of this land by these parties, they caused the same to be laid out into building lots, with streets and alleys, and called the same Port Schuyler.

Previous to the time of the purchase of this plot of ground by the Port Schuyler Company and naming the same Port Schuyler, this locality was known as the village of Washington. The date of the settlement of the village of Washington was previous to 1814, for in that year the first church located in this vicinity (Reformed Dutch Church) was organized at a meeting held in a school-house situated in the village of Washington, as appears from the records of this church.

Gibbonsville was that part of the present village of West Troy which lies between Port Schuyler, on the south, and Buffalo street, on the north, and was originally the farm of James Gibbons, a merchant of the city of Albany, and was by Mr. Gibbons laid out into building lots, with streets and alleys, and named Gibbonsville.

The village of Gibbonsville proved to be quite a thriving settlement, and in the year 1824 was duly incorporated as a village, and remained as such until the year 1836, when the act of its incorporation was repealed by the provisions of the act which incorporated the village of West Troy.

West Troy (previous to 1836) was that part of the present village which lies north of Buffalo street (the north boundary of Gibbonsville) and south of the present boundary line, which is the northern corporate limits of this village, and is the old line that divided the farms of John Bleeker and Volkert Oothout.

This West Troy was originally the farm of John Bleeker, and in the year 1823 was purchased of him by a number of capitalists, who called themselves the "West Troy Company." The deed which conveyed this parcel of land was executed on November 12, 1823, by John Bleeker and Elizabeth, his wife, and conveys about 400 acres of land, and excepts therefrom the Troy and Schenectady turnpike (now Genesee street), and lands occupied by the canal, and a parcel of land of about $\frac{8}{10}$ of an acre which then belonged to Thomas Schrimpton. This deed conveyed this land to George Tibbetts, Nathan Warren and Richard Hart, of Troy, and Philip Schuyler, of Saratoga, as trustees, and states that the above-named parties, together with Esaias Warren, Stephen Warren, Jacob Merritt, George Vail, Samuel Gale, Ebenezer Wiswall, Elias Pattison, Philip Hart, Jr., John D. Dickinson, John P. Cushman, John Pain, Theodore F. French and William Hart, have formed an association for the purpose of improving the premises, etc.

The consideration price named in this deed is $45,000. The eastern part of this parcel of land (the part which lies east of West street) was laid out into building lots, with street and alleys, and the western part was made into large lots, called "farm lots," which contained from 10 to 20 acres each. At present the greater part of these farm lots have been divided into building lots, and are covered with buildings. At the date of the purchase of this land by the West Troy Company, the only building thereon of any importance was a small two-story wooden tavern. This tavern had a piazza along the front and was located on the west side of the road, now known as Broadway, a short distance south of what is now called Central avenue (formerly Canal street), and stood upon the same plot of ground which is now occupied by the row of brick stores which are owned by Mr. Thomas Rath, and called "Rath's Block." This tavern, as early as 1824, was a very old building, and was probably erected at the time of, or previous to, the Revolutionary War. In 1830 this tavern was kept by one Samuel Ford.

Previous to the date of the incorporation of this village, the villages of Gibbonsville and West Troy were rivals, and although they lay side by side, they laid out their streets and named them without regard to each other, and consequently what is now known as Broadway was then called Water street, while within the limits of Port Schuyler and Gibbonsville; but when this street ran into West Troy, it was called Broad street. What is now called Washington street was then known as Washington street only in Gibbonsville, and in West Troy it was known as Rochester street. Of course, this created much confusion, especially with strangers.

By the Act of Legislature, in 1836, which incorporated the village of West Troy, all real and personal property which then belonged to the then village of Gibbonsville became the property of the village of West Troy; and by this act the village was divided into four wards, and the inhabitants residing in such wards, and duly qualified to vote, were directed to meet on the first Tuesday in May, 1836, at some proper place in each ward, at 9 o'clock in the forenoon, pursuant to a proper notice to be given and signed by the Trustees of the said village of Gibbonsville, and to then and there elect by ballot, in each of these wards, two trustees, who shall be electors and freeholders. Alva W. Rockwell, David D. Abrams and Albert S. Blackman were appointed by this act to attend and preside as inspectors of election of the First ward; Isaac Chapman, Martin Witbeck and John C. Green, in the Second ward; Samuel E. Ford, John T. Van Alstyne and Andrew Meneely, in the Third ward, and Abel W. Richardson, Abraham Van Arnam, Jr., and Alexander S. Lobdell, in the Fourth ward. All of the above-named persons were at this time among the most prominent business men of the village, but all are now deceased. These inspectors were directed to declare the persons receiving the greatest number of votes in their respective wards duly elected. This act also directed the said electors at the same time to elect a president for the said village.

Although the village of West Troy has grown very much since the time of its incorporation, and has in fact for some years past overrun the corporate limits, still the present corporate limits and the number and boundaries of the respective wards remain the same as designated in the charter of 1836. After the incorporation of this village it grew quite rapidly, although it was a thriving town before that time. The United States had, in 1813, purchased and located an arsenal in Gibbonsville, and the Erie Canal had run through the place since 1823, and was then (1836) being enlarged. The United States purchased the land upon which this arsenal was located from James Gibbons and Esther, his wife. This purchase comprised a plot of about twelve acres, fronting upon the Hudson River. The deed describes it as commencing at a point in the north line of Beaver street, at low water mark in the Hudson River, and conveys the land lying south of the north line of Beaver street, and between the Hudson River, on the east, and Albany street, on the west. There are now no maps that show this street called Beaver street; but by this deed it included and conveyed said street, which then ran in a westerly direction from the river. This deed conveyed this land in fee to the people of the United States, and to its successors or assigns, but reserved the right of a ferry privilege upon the river, and forbade the purchasers or their successors or assigns from ever maintaining a ferry from this parcel of land; it also reserved the right to said Gibbons to use the bed of a certain creek which ran through this land as a bed for a canal which was then proposed to be constructed (the Erie Canal). It was the intention of Mr. Gibbons that this creek be used for a canal and as a means of access for boats from the canal to the river, and *vice versa*. This creek was never used for such purpose, but at a point about half a mile further south, and in the then village of Washington, or Port Schuyler, such a canal was constructed, and is now know as the "lower side-cut." In the year 1828 the United States purchased of Esther Gibbons, as executrix of James Gibbons, deceased, another parcel of land which contained about thirty acres, and adjoined the land purchased in 1813 on the south and west. This last mentioned parcel of land Mr. Gibbons had contracted to sell to the United States, but died before the purchase was consummated. The purchase price of the first mentioned twelve acres was $2,585.00, and that of the other thirty acres was $9,622.00.

The village of Gibbonsville was laid out into village lots, with streets and alleys, in the year 1828, by Evert Van Allen, a civil engineer, although a portion thereof must have been mapped out as early as 1813, as appears by the deed of Gibbons and wife to the United States, which mentions the street called Beaver street, also a street called Albany street.

The original owners or proprietors of the villages of Port Schuyler, Gibbonsville and West Troy had large ideas as to the future greatness of these villages. They intended making them great commercial centers for the transfer and storage of all commodities to be carried on the canals and river. The proprietors of West Troy constructed a canal, in connection with the Erie Canal, which commenced at the south side of the side-cut at Union street, and midway between Broadway and the Erie Canal, which ran from this point south to the north side of Genesee street, where it then turned and ran into the Erie Canal; at the point where it ran into the Erie Canal was constructed a dry-dock, which was so constructed that boats would run on to a submerged platform, and then the boat and platform were raised out of the water by means of large screws, which connected with the platform and were worked with long levers. This canal was filled up several years ago. The proprietors of West Troy also contemplated and made provision for another canal in laying out the streets of the village. This proposed canal was to begin at the west side of the Erie Canal, at Union street, and then run through Union street until it reached West street; then run south through West street until it reached the south side of Genesee street, where it was then to turn to the east and run into Burlington street; and thence through Burlington street south to Canal street (now Central avenue); and thence east through Canal street to the Erie Canal. This canal was never constructed, and this is the reason why Union, Burlington and Canal streets are now so much wider than the other streets of the village.

In the village of Gibbonsville there was constructed a short canal or basin, which ran midway between Washington street and the canal, from the south side of Ferry street to the north side of Schenectady street. This basin was called the "Gibbonsville Basin," and was connected with the Erie Canal by means of a short cut or opening which ran along the south side of Ferry street. This basin was filled up within a few years after its construction.

VILLAGES OF GIBBONSVILLE AND WEST TROY.

The Legislature of the State of New York, on April 23, 1824, passed an "act to vest certain powers and privileges in the freeholders and inhabitants of the village of Gibbonsville," which act was shortly thereafter amended, and, on the first Tuesday of May, 1825, in accordance with the provisions of said acts, an election was held for the purpose of electing five trustees and one treasurer and collector. The persons elected were as follows:

Trustees, Julius Hanks, Elijah Ranney, Isaac Chapman, Edward Learned and Isaac Frink; Treasurer, Gerrit T. Lansing; Collector, Nathan Robbins. At the first meeting of the trustees they proceeded to choose one of the members of their body to be President of the Board, and the choice fell upon Julius Hanks. At a subsequent meeting of this Board they adopted certain village ordinances and ordered "that the same be published by affixing to the house of Abraham Van Arnam, with the President's name thereto affixed, together with the seal of the corporation."

At the annual meeting held in the said village of Gibbonsville, in 1826, the following persons

THE VILLAGE OF WEST TROY.

were elected trustees: Edward Learned, Abijah Wheeler, William G. Groesbeck, Thomas H. Dyer and Isaac Chapman. At this same meeting it was moved and carried that the trustees be empowered to raise seventy-five dollars, by tax, for the purpose of procuring fire hooks and ladders; for the construction of pumps and repairs thereof; for the erection of a pound (should such be required), and the surplus to be appropriated toward contingent expenses of the village.

The trustees of Gibbonsville, elected each succeeding year, were as follows, the first named in each instance being chosen as president at the first meeting of the Board:

1827—Elijah Ranny, Edward Learned, Isaac Chapman, James T. Morrison, Moses Tyler.

1828—Amos Larcom, Moses Tyler, William G. Groesbeck, David Morrison, Isaac H. Williams.

1829—Daniel T. Wandell, Isaac Chapman, David Wheeler, Moses Tyler, Charles Learned.

1830—Jonathan H. Dyer, Hiram M. Hopkins, Levi Lincoln, Moses Tyler, James T. Morrison.

1831—Isaac Chapman, Ephriam Baldwin, Hiram M. Hopkins, William P. Hall, David Wheeler.

1832.—William G. Groesbeck, Moses Tyler, Smith Ballou, Jonathan H. Dyer, Zachariah Craver.

1833—Isaac Chapman, Henry Thalhimer, Zachariah Craver, John Tisdall, Leonard Hannum.

1834—Isaac Chapman, Charles Learned, John B. Chollar, Eben Jones, Benjamin Brown.

1835—Edward Learned, Martin Witbeck, David Morrison, John C. Green, Jonathan H. Dyer.

At a meeting of the last-named trustees, held March 16, 1836, they adopted a resolution praying the Legislature to grant the act which incorporated the village of West Troy, and which was passed April 30, 1836; and in pursuance of this act these trustees called an election for May 3, 1836, at which the first trustees and president of the village of West Troy were elected. The whole number of votes polled at this election was 476. The following named officers were duly elected at this date: President, Edward Learned; Trustees, First ward, Thomas Evans, Jonathan Hart; Second ward, Isaac Chapman, Hiram M. Hopkins; Third ward, Samuel E. Ford, Henry Kimberly; Fourth ward, Abram Van Arnam, Jr., Joseph Twist. The presidents elected in each succeeding year were as follows: 1837, Martin Witbeck; 1838, Miron R. Peak; 1839, Andrew Meneely; 1840, Martin Witbeck; 1841, Samuel Wilgus; 1842, Miron R. Peak; 1843, Andrew Meneely; 1844, Albert T. Dunham; 1845, Albert Richards; 1846, Archibald A. Dunlop; 1847, Albert T. Dunham; 1848, Daniel C. Stewart; 1849, Heman Mather; 1850, Daniel C. Stewart; 1851, Samuel Crawford; 1852, Morgan L. Taylor; 1853, Lorenzo D. Collins; 1854, George B. Fraser; 1855-56, Martin Witbeck; 1857, Samuel H. Waterman; 1858, James Roy; 1859, James Brady; 1860, George R. Meneely; 1861, William Oswald; 1862, Peter A. Rogers; 1863, James Duffy; 1864-65, Francis Beebe; 1866-67, James Hamil; 1868, William B. Williams; 1869, Terrence Cummings; 1870-71, Perry Robinson; 1872, Joseph M. Lawrence; 1873, Terrence Cummings; 1874-75, Michael Riley; 1876-77, Patrick Lane; 1878, Robert P. Tunnard; 1879-80, Joseph McLean; 1881, George B. Mosher; 1882, John H. Hulsapple; 1883, William E. Cox; 1884, Patrick Lane; 1885, Terrence Cummings. The term of office being for one year.

CANALS.

The Erie Canal, which runs through this village, was authorized by an act of the Legislature of this State, passed April 15, 1817, and the work of construction was commenced July 4, 1817, and completed October 26, 1825, at a cost of $7,143,789.86.

The enlargement was authorized by an act of Legislature, passed May 11, 1835, the work of enlarging being commenced in August, 1836, the cost of which was $36,495,535.00.

The Champlain Canal, which extends from Lake Champlain to its junction with the Erie Canal, a short distance north of this village, was authorized by an act of Legislature, passed April 17, 1817, the work of construction being commenced June 10, 1818, and completed to the village of Waterford, Saratoga County, November 28, 1822, and fully completed on September 10, 1823, at a cost of $875,000, exclusive of the cost of the feeder at Glen's Falls.

At the date of the completion of the Erie Canal, in 1825, it was very small in comparison with its present size; it was then only forty feet wide and four feet deep; boats when loaded could not draw more than three and a half feet of water. The boats were also very small, being about eighty feet long and fourteen and a half feet wide, and could only carry about one-fourth as much freight as the largest boats in present use.

In 1837 the enlargement of the Erie Canal was made in this village; its depth was increased to seven feet, by means of removing eighteen inches of earth from the bottom, and raising the banks the same number of inches; the width was also increased to seventy feet, by removing thirty feet of earth from the east side of the original bank. In the early years of the canal the principal business done thereon was the carrying of passengers, the boats being provided with large cabins at both ends for their accommodation, the center portion being used for freight and baggage. These boats could only carry about forty or fifty tons of freight. At this time nearly all the boats were owned and run by capitalists, who formed themselves into companies, called "lines." At this time the passenger travel was very large, as this mode of traveling was much pleasanter and cheaper than by stage coach. None of the line boats carried horses on their boats, but were towed by horses, kept at convenient points along the canal where each line had its stables and horses for that purpose. It was no uncommon sight to see a whole family, with their household effects, load the same upon a boat and take passage for the west, whither they were emigrating; also, large parties of foreign emigrants, bound for the west, would pass through this village on board these passenger boats, and they would sit upon the decks, with different musical instruments, which they had brought with them, and play and sing their native melodies as they passed through the village. As a general rule, all first-class passengers going to or from the city of Albany did not pass through this village, but would leave or take the boats, as the case might be, at the village of Schenectady, there being a regular line of stage coaches that ran from Albany to Schenectady for that purpose; the reason being that the route was much shorter, besides much time was lost in locking the boats through the several locks between this village and the village of Cohoes. Among the first boats run upon the canals were the boats called bateaux, which had formerly run upon the Mohawk River between Schenectady and Utica and intermediate points, for carrying freight; these boats were pointed at both ends, and were about sixty feet long and nine or ten feet wide. Prior to about the year 1840 many of the canal boats that ran upon the Hudson River were provided with movable masts, rigging and sails, which would be set up after the boat had been locked into the river.

The business of towing canal boats upon the Hudson River, by means of steam-tugs or boats, was not introduced until about the year 1845. Previous to this date it had been the general custom to transfer the freight from the canal boats, either at Troy or Albany, to large boats called barges, and in that manner take all freight to New York and intermediate points upon the river; the barges being towed by steam tow-boats. The first regular line of canal boats that ran through from Buffalo to New York City was established and run by William C. Rice, of Troy, in 1845.

In 1825 the place for weighing canal boats, called the Weighlock, was located on the south side of Union street, a short distance west of Broadway. The weighlock building was a small wooden structure, and the mode of ascertaining the weight of a boat was to run the same into a large stone reservoir, or lock, which was connected with the canal by means of a gate, and then close the gate, when the water which was then in this large reservoir or lock was drawn off into a small reservoir, located below the level of the large lock, and the water thus drawn off was measured, and from the measurement thereof the weight of the boat and cargo was ascertained. This mode of weighing did not prove a success, as it was very inaccurate, and a few years thereafter it was abandoned and the mode of weighing by means of scales was adopted; by this last-mentioned mode, when the water was drawn from the lock, the boat rested upon a framework made of timber which was suspended upon heavy chains, and these chains were connected to an iron beam, which ran overhead from the lock into the office or building, where it was connected with a platform, upon which were placed iron weights, the beam being so balanced that a weight of $31\frac{1}{4}$ lbs. upon this platform represented the weight of one ton upon the frame in the lock upon which the boats rested. In weighing a boat by this last-mentioned mode, it was necessary to put on or take off these heavy iron weights used upon the platform, according to the weight of the boat and cargo, if loaded, and in some cases, in the weighing of one boat, it was necessary to handle seventy or more of these heavy weights.

This mode was more accurate than the former method, but it required much time and labor on account of the necessity of handling the heavy weights; this mode remained in use until 1853, when the present weighlock was built, at the northern terminus of this village, and the present easy mode of weighing by means of weights sliding upon scale beams was introduced.

Although the Erie Canal was not fully completed from Buffalo to Albany until October, 1825, yet as early as October, 1823, it was so far completed as to allow the running of boats from this village to Rochester, as is shown by an account of the same published in *The Troy Sentinel* of October 10, 1823, as follows:

"The opening of the Erie Canal on Wednesday, the 8th of October, 1823, was celebrated by the people of Troy in the following practical manner. When the procession of boats from the junction of the western and northern canals had passed on to Albany, according to the order of arrangements previously made, the *Trojan Trader*, a western freight boat, came down to the bridge near the Gibbonsville (West Troy) basin, opposite this city, and took on board the first load of merchandise sent from the Hudson west on the Erie Canal. The goods had been purchased several days and were only waiting for the navigation to be opened. As the occasion was new and interesting to us here, our merchants took some little pains to manifest their gratification. As the side-cut into the river opposite to Troy was not yet done, and as the junction canal, though completed and filled with water, could not yet be opened, so as to permit the *Trojan Trader* to come around by Waterford, down the Hudson, to be loaded at the wharf, it became necessary to transport the goods on wheels across the river to the place of embarkation on the main trunk of the canal. Accordingly, in the morning, this necessity being intimated to the carmen of Troy, with an alacrity highly honorable to their public spirit, they volunteered their services with one accord, to take the goods over. After loading their teams, they proceeded in two divisions to the two ferries, and being, through the liberality of Mr. Vanderhyden, the proprietor of the two ferries, taken across in his horse boats, toll free, they had the goods all on the bank of the canal by twelve o'clock. Several of our citizens lent their assistance to load the boat, and at two o'clock, the *Trader* having on board upward of twenty-five tons of merchandise, with her flag flying, and amid the cheers of assembled Trojans, started for the west. The *Trojan Trader* is commanded by Captain Brace; she is bound for Rochester, and on her flag are painted the following words: '*From Troy; the first western boat loaded at Hudson River.*'

THE VILLAGE OF WEST TROY.

There were between eight and ten tons of merchandise which the *Trader* could not take; these were put on board *The Troy*, another western boat, owned at Auburn."

The side-cut opposite to Troy, and known as the upper side-cut, was completed on Saturday, November 15, 1823. In the afternoon the locks were in readiness, the water was let in, and the packet-boat *Superior*, with a large party of citizens on board, passed through and crossed the river to Troy. Two freight-boats followed the *Superior*, and unloaded their cargoes at the river wharves of Troy, one being laden with staves, and the other with wheat.

Another very interesting event in connection with the Erie Canal took place in this village in 1824, this being a visit, or rather the passing through this village, of General La Fayette on Saturday, September 18, 1824, at the time of his memorable visit at Troy, and is thus described in *The Sentinel* of September 21 of that year: "*Reception of La Fayette in Troy.*—On Saturday last Troy had the happiness to receive La Fayette. The day was uncommonly serene, and the ceremonies were appropriate and interesting. Indeed, considering the uncertainty that existed until Friday concerning the time of the General's arrival and stay among us, the committee are entitled to very emphatic praise. The General, accompanied by his suite, the Governor of the State of New York and his suite, and the Mayor and Corporation of the City of Albany, came up from Albany on the canal, in the packet-boat *Schenectady*. He was expected as early as ten o'clock, but it had been found impossible by the Albany Committee to depart from their city sufficiently early for that purpose. At half-past one, however, the cannon at the United States Arsenal in Gibbonsville (West Troy) announced his approach in a national salute, and at two o'clock he reached the side-cut. There he was met by a deputation from the Troy Committee of Arrangements, and the packet-boat *Schenectady*, with all on board, was taken down through the locks into the river. Near the mouth of the side-cut, eight boats were waiting to tow the *Schenectady* across to the city. The boats were each fitted with a mast, on which was hoisted the national flag; each was furnished with four strong oarsmen, and in the stern of each, to guide the movement, sat the master of the sloop to which the boat belonged. The boats, being arranged in line and connected by hawsers, took the *Schenectady* in tow, and pulling out into the river far enough to clear the point of the shoal that stretches along the south side of the channel leading from the lock, they turned with a graceful sweep down the river, and gave to view the beautiful line in its whole length. After the General with his retinue had passed the United States Arsenal on his way to the side-cut, five beautiful uniformed companies from Albany, who had escorted him from that city, crossing at the ferry, united with the military of Troy, and the whole were paraded in Ferry street to wait his landing."

FERRIES.

At the time of the incorporation of this village (1836) there were two ferries—one at the foot of Ferry street, called the Gibbonsville Ferry; the other at the foot of Canal street (now Central avenue), called the West Troy Ferry. Previous to about this date, this last-mentioned ferry was owned by one Derrick Y. Vanderheyden, of Troy, and was called the Vanderheyden Ferry, and was purchased by the West Troy Company about this date from Mr. Vanderheyden. The ferry-boats were then propelled by means of horse power, the horses being on the boats and created the power which moved the paddles. These boats had no cabins or other covering, and only a few wooden benches for the accommodation of passengers. They could carry about six teams of horses, with their wagons. The rates charged were twelve and a half cents for single horse and wagon; nineteen cents for team of horses and wagon; passengers, three cents each. During the winter months these rates were doubled in case the boats were able to run. These horse-ferry-boats which for many years plied between this village and Troy were first placed upon the river in May, 1819, and the first boat introduced and used is referred to in the *Troy Budget* of June the first, as follows: "The Horse-Boat invented by Mr. Langdon has been in operation at Mr. Van Derheyden's ferry in this city during last week. The machinery is built upon a common scow. The boat crosses the river, which is less than a quarter of a mile, in four minutes. It is confidently expected that for the purpose of dispatch and on the ground of economy this boat will be in high repute and general use throughout the United States."

The ferry above referred to as the West Troy Ferry was established by Derrick Van der Heyden, but at what date cannot be ascertained, but it is supposed to have been soon after he purchased the land or farm upon which the City of Troy is now situated, in 1707; and in the year 1794 this ferry was being conducted by his son, Jacob D. Van Derheyden. This ferry at the present time is principally owned and conducted by Mr. George Mark, of the town of Watervliet, and from papers in his possession, which contain a sworn statement made by Cornelius Marshall, it appears that in 1777 the American troops which took an active part in the battle at Stillwater between the American troops under Gen. Gates and the British troops under Gen. Burgoyne crossed at this ferry. The troops were ferried across by means of lashing together flat-boats, called bateaux. Mr. Marshall was at this time employed at this ferry, and was 14 years of age.

In 1807 Daniel T. Wandell, of Troy, established and ran a ferry, called the "Middle Ferry," which ran from a point in this village, then Gibbonsville, near Buffalo street, to a point on the Troy side of the river, a short distance south of Division street, at the homestead of Mr. Wandell. In the year 1810 Mr. Wandell sold this ferry to Derrick Y.

Vanderheyden, who thereupon discontinued it. For several years previous to 1834 Mr. Wandell was the general superintendent of the West Troy Ferry and the Gibbonsville Ferry, they being at that time the only ferries running. The first ferry-boat run by steam power was run at the West Troy Ferry by Mr. Wandell about the year 1833, but it did not prove a success, and was soon abandoned. Soon after the purchase of the Vanderheyden Ferry by the West Troy Company this company also purchased the Gibbonsville Ferry, and discontinued it, the object of the company being to compel the travel to come further up town, and thereby build up and increase the value of the real estate owned by this company.

At the present time there are three steam passenger ferries running between this village and the City of Troy, the oldest of these ferries being the one heretofore referred to as running from the foot of Central avenue, and is now commonly called the "Mark Ferry;" another, running from the pier or extreme southerly point of Green Island, near the foot of Union street, in this village. This ferry is owned and run by Messrs. Thomas Rath, John Reily and Joseph McLean. The other one, running from a point a short distance north of North street, near the United States Arsenal. This ferry is now owned and run by Messrs. Clark W. Delano and Frederick T. Hathaway.

The large highway iron bridge, which connects this village with Troy, running from the foot of Genesee street in this village to the foot of Congress street in that city, was erected by the Troy and West Troy Bridge Company. This company was incorporated by a special act of legislature, passed April 23, 1872; the work of construction was commenced on the 12th day of September of that year, and the bridge completed October 1, 1874; the total cost of bridge and approaches being $350,000.

SAILING VESSELS ON THE RIVER.

Previous to 1850 the greater portion of the freight carried upon the Hudson river was by sailing vessels, which were called "sloops," "schooners," or "scows," according to their size and manner of construction. The business of carrying passengers by sailing vessels was abandoned as early as 1836. A very large business in the transfer and sale of lumber was carried on at this village from 1832 to 1845, the lumber coming down the canal on canal boats, and being unloaded here it would then be reloaded upon the sailing vessels for shipment down the river. About one hundred and thirty vessels were engaged in this business at this village. The river docks where they were loaded were north of Genesee street and south of Buffalo street; the river front lying between these two streets was not at that time filled in and docked so that boats could load and unload therefrom.

This village was the home of many of the owners and captains of these sailing crafts, of which the following were the most important:

Sloops—American Banner, Capt. Thomas Rafferty; Active, Capt. Butler Hubbard; Burlington, Capt. Silas Betts; Samuel Brewster, Capt. Andrew Hitchcock; Belvedere, Capt. Peter Hicks; Commodore Rogers, Capt. James Warford; Clarissa, Capt. George Collins; Clinton, Capt. Robert Robinson; Currier, Capt. Thomas Anderson; Conveyance, Capt. Stephen Washburn, Sr.; David D. Crane, Capt. Asahel W. Gilbert; Don Ramone, Capt. Harlow Rhodes; Fox, Capt. Stephen Washburn, Sr.; Henry Gage, Capt. William Lobdell; Highlander, Capt. Wm. Crawford; James North, Capt. William Foot; Juno, Capt. John Silliman; Kinderhook, Capt. James Warford; Leader, Capt. William Wood; Jane McCoy, Capt. Andrew Foster; Martha Ann, Capt. James Hardy; Minerva, Capt. John King; William Mayo, Capt. Meneely Hitchcock; Mechanic, Capt. Isaac Hubbard; North America, Capt. Daniel Curtis; Miriam, Capt. Isaac R. Getty; Pilot, Capt. John King; Ranger, Capt. David King; Peter Ritter, Capt. Charles Mead; Superior, Capt. Isaac R. Getty; Shepherdess, Capt. Patrick Lamb; Senator, Capt. Isaac Hitchcock; Pierre Van Cortlandt, Capt. Jacob Young; Robert Wiltsey, Capt. William Harvey; John Ward, Capt. Alfred Mosher.

Schooners—Thomas H. Benton, Capt. John Garrahan; Ballston, Capt. William Wood; Cadmus, Capt. Andrew Hitchcock; Eleanor, Capt. John Evertsen; Isaac Merritt, Capt. James Wood; Mary Anna, Capt. Asahel W. Gilbert; Meridan, Capt. Henry Evertsen; Miller, Capt. Medad Wood; Commodore Porter, Capt. Richard McLaughlin; Regulator, Capt. Henry Finch; Andrew Stewart, Capt. Asahel W. Gilbert; David Smith, Capt. James Farrell; Stranger, Capt. Edward Lane; Ann S. Salter, Capt. Asahel W. Gilbert; Caleb Wright, Capt. Jonathan Patridge.

Scows—Grampus, Capt. Washington Mowry; Hercules, Capt. James Hitchcock; Ohio, Capt. Hiram Tinslar; United States, Capt. Stephen Washburn, Jr.; Globe, Capt. James Hillis.

Of the captains above mentioned only a few now remain residents of this village, the greater number having died, while a few have removed; and of those now living and residing here may be mentioned Isaac R. Getty and Asahel W. Gilbert.

Captain Getty was born at Lansingburgh, Rensselaer County, N. Y., November 24, 1807, and began to run upon the river when 17 years of age, and came to this village to reside in 1838. He followed the river for fifty-five years, and is now the oldest river captain residing in this village. At different times during the period of 55 years which he was upon the river he was master of seven different sailing vessels and eleven different steam vessels.

Captain Gilbert was born in Troy in 1819, and followed the river from 1829 to 1870; he came to this village to reside in 1845. During the time he followed the river he was at different periods captain of ten different sailing vessels and five steam vessels. He also built and sold a number of sailing crafts.

THE VILLAGE OF WEST TROY.

LOCAL NAMES IN THE VILLAGE.

By common consent of the inhabitants of this village, different localities in the village have obtained local names, such as "Port Shad," "Temperance Hill," "Shanghai," and "Durinsville."

"Port Shad," being the extremes outherly part of the village, obtained the title a number of years ago by reason of the large number of shad that was caught there.

"Temperance Hill" is that part of the high ground in this village which lies west of the Erie Canal and between the United States Arsenal and Buffalo street. About the year 1838 there was a great temperance movement in this village, and a temperance society formed with about 1,700 members. This society decided to give a grand Fourth of July picnic, and selected this hill as the place to hold it. The picnic was a great success, and at the dinner one of the prominent members, Mr. Lewis Rousseau, proposed that the hill upon which they were holding the entertainment should be called "Temperance Hill," and thereafter, by common consent, this name was adopted by the residents of this village. At the time of the holding of this picnic that part of the village west of the canal was vacant ground, there being only about a half a dozen buildings erected west of the canal.

"Shanghai" is the name of that part of this village which is west of William street in the vicinity of Union street. This name originated several years ago from the fact that one Daniel Carthy, who owned considerable property, and resided in this vicinity, was very fond of fancy poultry, and he introduced and raised the first Shanghai roosters in the village, and they were a great curiosity to the residents, who transferred the name of the fowl to the locality.

"Durinsville" is that part of this village which lies west of and in the vicinity of the Erie Canal, at the extreme northern part of the village. This name originated several years ago from the name of a family called Durin, who resided in that vicinity.

Another local name, which is now only a matter of history, is that of "Stone Hook." This name was given to a group of rocks which stood on the bank of the river at and near the foot of Buffalo street. These rocks were not very large, but were very prominent by reason of their being the only rocks or high ground for some distance upon the west bank of the river. They were removed a number of years ago. The residence of Mr. John I. Winne, upon the southeast corner of Broadway and Buffalo street, now called the "Rock House," is built upon one of these rocks, and thus obtained its name. This group of rocks was also called "Steen-Hoeck" and "Stony Point" as well as "Stone Hook." This name was in use as early as 1675, and was used as a point of locality in conveyances of real estate on the opposite bank of the river. Stonehook Creek was the original name of the creek which runs through this village, and now called Dry River.

CHURCHES.

The first church ever organized and located within the limits which now comprise this village was the "Reformed Protestant Dutch Church of Washington and Gibbonsville," organized by the Classis of Albany in the year 1814. The first record of this organization reads as follows: "At a meeting held in the school-house in the village of Washington, agreeably to notice, for the purpose of electing elders and deacons to manage the concerns of a church to be organized, Peter S. Schuyler was chairman, and Volkert D. Oathout clerk. Peter S. Schuyler and Volkert D. Oathout were elected elders, and Samuel Phillips and Stephen Conger deacons. Dated March 19, 1814." The consistory of this church united with that of the Reformed Dutch Church, located on the Boght, in the town of Watervliet, and called the Rev. Robert Bronk, who preached alternately in these churches—the services here being held in the old school-house. This building still stands on the rear of the lot of Mr. James Forsyth on Broadway, near the present brick school-house. The actual organization of this church dates from Sunday, March 22, 1814, when, immediately after divine service, held in the old school-house, upon which occasion Rev. Mr. Bradford, of Albany, preached, the above-named persons were ordained, according to the forms of the Reformed Dutch Church. The salary of the Rev. Mr. Bronk as pastor of this church was $300, to be paid semi-annually. Mr. Bronk continued his labors as pastor of these two churches for about ten years, when he resigned his charge of the church at the Boght, and devoted his whole time to this church until 1834, when he resigned on account of ill health. Directly after the organization, this congregation made a move to build a church, and on July 10, 1816, the first church was dedicated, the corner-stone having been laid in April, 1815. This edifice was erected upon a plot of ground now occupied by a brick dwelling owned by Mrs. Mansion, located on the west side of Broadway, about three hundred feet north of North street, and cost $5,568. This plot of ground was donated by John Schuyler, Jr., and James Gibbons. The Rev. John Woods became the next pastor of this church, but remained only a few months. The services were irregularly conducted by different ministers until the spring of 1838, when the Rev. Oscar H. Gregory, D. D., became pastor. Owing to the fact that the greater portion of the congregation of this church were residents of that portion of the village north of the United States Arsenal, it was decided to build a new and more convenient house of worship. In 1838 a lot on the northwest corner of Washington and Buffalo streets was selected as a site for the new church. In August, 1839, the corner-stone for the new church was laid by Rev. Oscar H. Gregory, D. D., and the next year the new church was dedicated, the sermon at the dedicatory service being preached by Rev. Dr. Wyckoff, of Albany. The cost of this edifice was $12,922. For a few years services were held in the old church, commonly called the "South Church," in the morning, and in the afternoon and evening in the new church, commonly called the "North Church." In 1844 the parish was divided, and the old church, on account of financial embarrassment, was sold by order of the Court of Chancery, and was purchased by Hon. Clarkson F. Crosby, and thus ended the original organization known as the "Reformed Protestant Dutch Church of Washington and Gibbonsville."

On the 18th day of June, 1884, the "South Reformed Protestant Dutch Church in the village of West Troy" was organized, with Philip S. Schuyler, Robert Dunlop and John C. Schuyler elders, and David Moore and Stephen C. Dermott deacons, with thirty-six other members, and the old church was then sold by Mr. Crosby to the new organization. In 1840 the "New Church," or "North Church," as it had been theretofore known, changed its name and corporate title to the "North Reformed Church of West Troy," and these churches thereafter became separate and distinct organizations, the Rev. Dr. Gregory remaining as the pastor of the North Reformed Church.

Trinity Church (Episcopal) was organized and incorporated in 1834. For two years previous to that time the Rev. Dr. David Butler and his assistant, of St. Paul's Episcopal Church of Troy, held mission services in a small wooden school-house on the west side of Burlington street, a short distance north of Union street; but two families formed the nucleus of the congregation, being those of Raymond Taylor and James Lobdell. The first vestry of Trinity Church was made up as follows: Rector, the Rev. James Tappan; Wardens, James Lobdell and A. S. Blackman; Vestrymen, Raymond Taylor, John Mason, Glover Blackman, Edgar Botsford, Gilbert C. Bedell, Thomas Evans, John Worthington and Jonathan Hart. The Rev. Mr. Tappan commenced his work here in June, 1834, and held service in Port Schuyler, Gibbonsville, and West Troy, the parish having no regular place for holding services. Mr. Tappan resigned in May, 1836, and in December of that year the Rev. William C. Cooley became rector, but only remained about ten months, during which time (1837) the first church edifice was erected. This was a brick building and was located on the west side of Salem street, between Middle and Spring streets. This church was consecrated on June 4, 1837, by the Rt. Rev. Bishop Onderdonk. In October, 1837, Rev. Mr. Lewis became rector of this parish, and remained as such until November, 1838.

Owing to the great distance and trouble of reaching the church edifice on Salem street, the people in the northern and central part of the village organized and incorporated a new church or parish, called St. Luke's, on November 19, 1838, and called the Rev. Washington Van Zandt as rector, who remained as such for the short time which this new parish remained a separate parish. In 1839 the Rev. Aliva T. Twing became rector of Trinity parish, and through his influence the parish of St. Luke's was abandoned and became again a part of Trinity parish. Dr. A. T. Twing remained two years, and was succeeded by Rev. William H. A. Bissell, who, on January 1, 1841, became the rector of the united parishes of Trinity Church and St. Luke's Chapel. The Rev. Mr. Bissell divided his time between Trinity and St. Luke's, the services of the latter being held in a building erected by St. Luke's parish, and situate on the north side of Canal street (now Central avenue), between Broadway and the Erie Canal. In 1844 the church edifice on Salem street was sold, and a few years afterward was destroyed by fire. After the sale of the church, all services were held at St. Luke's Chapel. In September, 1845, the Rev. Joshua Weaver became rector of the parish, and on January 10, 1848, the present church edifice was consecrated by the Rt. Rev. Bishop Alonzo Potter, of Pennsylvania. In April, 1851, Rev. Mr. Weaver resigned, and in May of the same year the Rev. Philander K. Cady became rector. During Mr. Cady's rectorship a parish school was established, which was successful during his rectorship, and for a number of years thereafter. Mr. Cady remained rector for six years, and was succeeded by Rev. Charles W. Homer, who remained until July, 1858.

On November 1, 1858, the Rev. George W. Hathaway became rector, and remained until July, 1863. On November 1, 1863, the Rev. Joseph S. Saunders became rector, and during his rectorship the three-story brick rectory, north of the church edifice, was built. In May, 1867, Mr. Saunders resigned. In August, 1867, the Rev. John Townsend was installed as rector, and after a service of six and one-half years, he resigned in February, 1874. In May, 1874, the Rev. Henry H. Oberly was installed as rector, and in 1879 resigned. In June, 1879, the Rev. George F. Breed became rector, and remained as such until January, 1883, when he resigned, and was succeeded in March by the Rev. E. Bayard Smith, the present incumbent. In 1875 a mission chapel in connection with this church was erected on Groton street, in the southern part of the village, and called St. Gabriel's Chapel. In 1878 a mission chapel in connection with this church was erected on Ford street, in the northern part of the village, and called St. Andrew's Chapel.

The present church edifice, which was erected in 1848, is a wooden building, which cost about $10,000. In 1865 this edifice was enlarged by adding a wing on the south side, and increasing the seating capacity about 100. In 1877 this edifice was still further enlarged by the addition of an organ chamber on the southeast corner.

In 1882 the present chapel was built, which is a two-story wooden building, and is situated upon the rear of the church lot, the second floor of this building being used as a chapel and Sunday school room, the first floor being divided into rooms for guild room, vestry room, etc. This chapel, with furniture, cost $2,000. The Sunday school of this parish is divided into three parts,

THE VILLAGE OF WEST TROY.

being the parish school, which holds its services in the church chapel, Mr. Wm. Hollands, Superintendent; St. Gabriel's Mission Sunday school, which holds its services at St. Gabriel's chapel, Mr. Edmund S. Hollands, Superintendent; and St. Andrew's Mission Sunday school, which holds its services at St. Andrew's chapel, Mr. John H. Hulsapple, Superintendent.

St. Patrick's Catholic Church of this village was organized in 1839. and the lot upon which this church was erected in 1840 was purchased April 20, 1839, and is located on the southwest corner of Union and Burlington streets. The first service held in this church was a mass, on Christmas day, 1840.

This church was organized by, and built under the supervision of, the Rev. John Shannahan, the priest then in charge of St. Peter's Church of Troy, N. Y.

The first priest in charge of this church was the Rev. James Quinn, who, at the time of its organization and building, was an assistant at St. Peter's Church, under the Rev. John Shannahan. The Rev. James Quinn was placed in charge of this parish as soon as the church was completed, and continued until June, 1845, when he was succeeded by the Rev. Thomas Martin, who remained in charge until May, 1848. The Rev. Father Martin was succeeded by the Rev. John Corry, who remained until February, 1849, when he was succeeded by the Rev. William McCallion.

In February, 1850, the Rev. Thomas A. Kyle was installed, and in or about this year he organized the church in the southern part of this village known as St. Bridget's Church.

The Rev. Father Kyle was succeeded in June, 1855, by the Rev. Thomas Daly, who remained until November, 1855, when he was succeeded by the Rev. William Fennelly.

The Rev. Wm. Fennelly remained until October, 1868. The present priest in charge of this parish, the Rev. William F. Sheehan, succeeded the Rev. Father Fennelly in October, 1868. The Rev. Father Sheehan is at present assisted in his labors by two assistant priests, the Rev. Francis Cunningham and Rev. Patrick Harrigan. The trustees of this church in 1843 were: Thomas Riley, Thomas O'Connor, Patrick Fitzsimmons, Michael Develin, James Keenan, Sr., James McGrath, James Brady and Michael Roe. In connection with this church is a parish school for boys, the teachers being the Sisters of Mercy. This school is conducted in a brick school-house, which adjoins the church edifice on the west.

The North Reformed Church of West Troy, as the reader has before learned, was built and organized in 1840, the corner-stone having been laid in August, 1839, the dedicatory sermon having been preached by Rev. Dr. Wyckoff, of Albany, and for a few years thereafter services on the Sabbath being held in the old, or South Church, in the morning, and in this church, which was then called the new, or North Church, in the evening.

In 1844 the Rev. O. H. Gregory discontinued holding services at the old South Church, and devoted his time exclusively to this church, holding services regularly each Sabbath. From 1844 to 1865 this church used as a consistory room a small wooden building, originally built for a seminary, which was located on the east side of Washington street, about fifty feet north of the Meneely Bell Foundry.

In 1865 the present brick chapel was erected, which adjoins the church edifice on the north. In 1854 the steeple of this church was blown off, and the bell broken, by a severe gale of wind.

The Rev. O. H. Gregory, D. D., became the pastor of this church from the date of its organization, and continued as such until the year 1870, when, by reason of his failing health, he was compelled to resign. In June, 1871, the Rev. Alfred J. Hutton became the pastor of this church, and remained as such until April 1, 1879, when he resigned. On December 1, 1879, the Rev. John G. Lansing became the pastor of this church, and remained such until August 1, 1884, when he resigned to fill the chair of the professorship of Hebrew at the Theological Seminary at New Brunswick, New Jersey.

The church edifice of this organization is the oldest in this village, and in 1882 it was thoroughly repaired, several alterations made, and an addition built on the west end for an organ loft, a new organ purchased, and the interior entirely refurnished, at an expense of $13,000.

The present pastor, the Rev. John Walter Beardslee, was installed December 1, 1884.

The South Reformed Protestant Dutch Church for its first pastor called the Rev. Theodore F. Wyckoff on July 25, 1844, and he remained until December 18, 1854. On May 16, 1855, the Rev. Garret L. Roof became pastor of this church, and remained until January 23, 1865, when he resigned. On May 10, 1865, the Rev. Jacob S. Wyckoff was installed, and continued as the pastor of this church until October 28, 1869. On the 16th day of March, 1870, the Rev. Selah W. Strong was installed as pastor of this church, and continued as such until the time of his decease, which occurred at the church parsonage on the 6th day of November, 1884, after the long pastorate of over fourteen years.

In the year 1871 this congregation found that the "old church" edifice was entirely unfitted for the demands of the growing congregation, and while the officers were debating as to the best plans to be adopted to obtain a more suitable edifice, the Hon. James B. Jermain sent to the consistory a communication, whereby he proposed to erect for the congregation, at his own expense, a church edifice upon the following among other conditions :

1st—A change of site, including the purchase of ground on the part of the congregation.

2d—The furnishing of the building, when completed, with all necessary furniture, including organ, etc., by the congregation.

3d—The edifice to be a "memorial building," in memory of Sylvanus P. Jermain (the father of Mr. James B. Jermain) and of his family.

This proposition was immediately accepted by the consistory, and the present site, on the northwest corner of Groton and Middle streets, was purchased for $6,000.

The ground was broken for the new church June 28, 1872, and it was completed in November, 1874, and dedicated December 30, 1874. This new church edifice or "memorial building" (now occupied by this congregation) is of stone, and of the style of architecture called the "early decorate Gothic," and cost about $100,000. This building is by far the finest church edifice in this village.

During the year 1874 the present elaborate tower was added to this building. In the year 1878 the present chapel, situated on the lots north of the "memorial building," was erected, which is a Gothic building of brick and stone, and cost, exclusive of furniture, $6,350, and was opened with appropriate services on Sunday evening, December 22, 1878. The parsonage, which is now located in the rear of the church, was erected upon the site now occupied by the "memorial building," and was moved westward some seventy feet, and enlarged and repaired at the time of the building of the "memorial building."

The Sunday school in connection with this church was organized in 1844, with twenty members, the exercises being held in the church until 1859, when a wooden chapel on the south of the old church edifice on Broadway was erected. The following is a list of those who have served successively as Superintendents of the School:

Miss Gertrude Ten Eyck, Clarkson F. Crosby, John M. Fort, Lewis Taylor, Adrian Winne, Lorenzo D. Lawrence, Rev. Jacob S. Wyckoff, Lorenzo D. Lawrence, James Campbell, Jr., John J. Clute, Rev. S. W. Strong, Edmund W. Johnson. During the year 1869 the infant department of this school was organized by Mrs. Stephen R. Schuyler and Miss Anna R. Jermain.

This church, in 1885, by a vote of a majority of its members, severed its relations to the Reformed Church, and became connected with the Presbytery of Albany.

St. Bridget's Catholic Church.—This church was built in 1850, under the supervision of Rev. Thomas Kyle, the priest then in charge of St. Patrick's Church of this village. This church is located on the northwest corner of Salem and Mansion streets. The Rev. William Cullinan was the first priest in charge of this church and parish, in the spring of 1854, and remained in charge until May, 1883.

The present priest in charge of this parish, the Rev. James A. Curtin, succeeded the Rev. Father Cullinan in May, 1883, and, in the following November, began to make extensive improvements in the church edifice, by the addition of a sacristy on the west, thereby doubling its seating capacity, and by purchasing a bell, and making several other improvements, at a cost of $18,000. In the fall of 1883 this church purchased the property on the southwest corner of Salem and Mansion streets, known as the "Sague property," the dwelling on the corner being at present used as a rectory, and the adjoining buildings on the south being used as a school and residence for the Sisters in charge of the school. This school is for the instruction of boys and girls in the ordinary English branches, and is under the charge of the Sisters of St. Joseph, and has an attendance of about 250 scholars. The Rev. James A. Curtin is assisted in his duties, as priest of this parish, by his brother, Rev. Daniel F. Curtin.

The Washington Street Methodist Episcopal Church.—This church was organized in April, 1831, the first trustees being Daniel T. Wandell, William Tucker, William P. Hall, Ammon Hammond and David I. Dutcher. Mr. L. Brown was elected clerk and Ammon Hammond treasurer. At this meeting it was resolved that the said trustees and their successors in office should forever thereafter be called and known by the name and title of the "Trustees of the Gibbonsville Station of the Methodist Episcopal Church in the town of Watervliet." The trustees of this church then purchased of Ebenezer Prescott a lot on the northwest corner of Washington and Ferry streets, and thereupon erected a small one-story wooden edifice, thirty-five feet front and forty-five feet deep. In 1840 this was enlarged by adding twenty feet in the depth, and by the erection of galleries. In 1841 a small wooden vestry was erected on the same lot on the north. This building was used as a Sunday school room until about 1857, when it was converted into a parsonage. In the spring of 1857 the old wooden church was sold and removed, and the corner-stone of the present church was laid, and it was completed so that the first service therein was held in January, 1858. This edifice cost about $9,000, and the furniture about $4,000. A steeple, bell and town clock were added to this edifice in 1883, and the parsonage enlarged and greatly improved, at a cost of about $8,000.

The old wooden church, which was removed in 1857, was purchased by Mr. John M. Jones, and by him taken down and removed to his carriage works, on the corner of Berlin and Circle streets, where it was re-erected, and is now used as a machine shop in connection with the Jones Horse Car Works. In the year 1849 a number of the members of this church, residing in the upper part of this village, organized a new church, known as the "Ohio Street Methodist Episcopal Church," and thereafter this church dropped the name of "Gibbonsville Station of the Methodist Episcopal Church," and became the "Washington Street Methodist Episcopal Church." In connection with this church is a Sunday school in prosperous condition. The infant department, being an important factor, was organized in 1843, and in that year Mr. James D. Lobdell became the superintendent, and continued in the office until the date of his decease in 1879. The present pastor of this church is the Rev. H. C. Farrer.

The Ohio Street Methodist Episcopal Church.—This church was organized, in the spring of 1849, by Alexander S. Lobdell, Ashael Potter, Edward Mallory, R. E. Gorton and Otis Wood. On June 5, 1849, the trustees of this church purchased the church property located on the southwest corner of

THE VILLAGE OF WEST TROY.

Ohio and Ontario streets in this village, known as the First Presbyterian or Congregational Church, and commonly called the "Bethel Church." This church edifice was a small wooden structure, and on November 19, 1849, was totally destroyed by fire. The first preacher assigned to this congregation was the Rev. I. F. Yates. Immediately after the destruction of the "Bethel," this congregation took action to rebuild the church, and in the following spring (1850) the corner-stone of the present church edifice was laid, and the building was completed soon after, which is a two-story brick structure, the auditorium being on the second floor and the Sunday school and class rooms on the first floor. For about thirty years this church was the only Protestant church in the northern part of this village. In 1881 the brick parsonage, which adjoins this church on the south, was erected. The present pastor is the Rev. H. Van Decar.

The "First Particular Baptist Church and Society of Gibbonsville and West Troy," commonly called the First Baptist Church, was organized at a meeting held March 14, 1827, at the residence of Thomas Shrimpton, which was located on the northwest corner of Broadway and Buffalo street, and was composed of seventeen members; the first trustees being Edward Learned, Thomas Shrimpton, Jonathan Caulkins, Hiram M. Hopkins and Cyrus Kenney. The first real property owned by this society is the same upon which the church and parsonage are now located, being the plot of ground situate on the northeast corner of Ohio street and Central avenue, and comprises four village lots. This land was given to the Society by Philip Schuyler and others, as trustees of the West Troy Company, by a deed dated July 4, 1827, upon the condition that the premises conveyed should be only used for church purposes by this society or its successors. The first church edifice was erected upon this plot of ground in 1829, and was a small wooden structure, which was used until 1842, when it was decided to erect a large edifice, and this building was removed and sold, and converted into a French Catholic Church. The second church edifice was erected in 1842, and was of brick, with a basement. This building fronted on Canal street, and cost about $1,000. It was used by this society until 1870, when it was torn down, and the present edifice was erected, which is of brick, and fronts on Ohio street. This building is of two stories, the auditorium being on the second floor, and the lecture room, study, etc., on the first floor. This edifice, with the furniture, cost upward of $20,000. Adjoining the present church edifice on the east is the parsonage, which was erected in 1847. The first pastor of this church was the Rev. Ashley Vaughan, who became such in July, 1830, and served for four years. This church has had several pastors, among them being the Rev. William Arthur, the father of ex-President Chester A. Arthur, who served as pastor from April, 1853, until April, 1856. The present pastor, the Rev. A. M. Prentice, was installed in September, 1877.

The Sunday school in connection with this church was organized in 1828, the first superintendent being Jonathan Caulkins, and the following persons having thereafter served successively as superintendents, viz.: Isaac I. Fonda, ——— Stearns, Merritt Potter, Miron R. Peak, Edwin S. Johnson, Miron R. Peak, Edwin S. Johnson, Henry C. Kelsey, Andrew G. Coats, David H. Simmons.

In the summer of 1867 this Sunday school organized a Mission Sunday school in the southern part of this village (Port Schuyler), the pastor of the church, the Rev. Edward Mills, being the superintendent, and, in 1868, was succeeded by Albert Tayer. This Mission school continued until 1875, when it was disbanded.

In the year 1869 the Sunday school of this church organized a Mission Sunday school in the village of Green Island, Edwin S. Johnson being the superintendent. This school continued as a mission school until 1873, when it became an independent organization. This school is now in a flourishing condition, and holds regular meetings at its rooms on the corner of Market and George streets, and retains the name of "The Baptist Mission."

The First Presbyterian Church.—This church was first organized at a meeting held in the school-house which was located on the west side of Burlington street, a short distance north of Union street, on the evening of February 12, 1834, and was presided over by the Rev. Marcus Smith (he being the first pastor of this church), and it was resolved that it be known by the name of the Presbyterian or Congregational Society of the village of West Troy. Hiram M. Hopkins, Horace L. Dann and Henry Kimberley were elected trustees. On the 27th of the same month this society organized itself into a "Congregational Church," this form of church government being preferred to that of the Presbyterian. On or about the first of September of this year the first house of worship of this congregation was completed, and was situated on the southwest corner of Ohio and Ontario streets. It was a small wooden building, and cost about $650. This edifice was familiarly called "The Bethel," this congregation making a special effort to secure the attendance and interest of boatmen, and when meetings were to be held at the church a flag was hoisted from its cupola as a signal to the boatmen. In 1835 the form of church government was changed from the Congregational to that of the Presbyterian, and the name of the "First Presbyterian Church of West Troy" was adopted. A year or two thereafter, this society again changed their form of church government to that of the Congregational. On the 26th of August, 1839, it was decided by this society to withdraw from the Congregational association and return to the Presbyterian, as organized in 1835, and unite with the "New School Presbytery of Troy, N. Y.," to which they were admitted on October 11, 1840. This society retained a regular pastor until July, 1845, but thereafter had no regular preaching or pastor (until reorganized in 1875), having services and preaching when temporary supplies could be obtained. This society, finding that it could not struggle on and maintain the church and a pastor, held a meeting on March 7, 1849, and decided to sell the "meeting house" and lots; and, on June 5 thereafter, this property was sold to the trustees of the Ohio Street Methodist Episcopal Church. This church or society remained dormant until 1872, when it was revived; but owing to the failure to properly elect trustees during the time the society remained dormant, it became necessary to reincorporate the society, which was formally accomplished on February 24, 1872. In the year 1875-76 the present church edifice, which is located on the north side of Union street, a short distance east of Ford street, was erected. This new church edifice is a two-story brick building; the total cost, including site, edifice and furniture, was $15,500.

The present pastor is the Rev. Charles G. Mattison.

The Church of the "Holy Heart of Mary" (French Catholic), corner of Stafford and Buffalo streets, was organized by the Rev. Eugene Rey, a native of France and member of a religious society or order of that country called the "Eudistes." The corner-stone of the church edifice was laid September 11, 1881.

Upon the front of the edifice was placed two stone tablets, which bore the following inscriptions: "Consécration de Jésus et Marie dite les Eudistes." "Eglise du Saint Cœur de Marie." Upon the corner-stone was inscribed as follows: "Pierre angulaire, posée le Septembre, 1881." In 1883 the Rev. Louis Leduce became the priest in charge of this church. On April 2, 1885, the church edifice was totally destroyed by fire, at a loss of $18,000.

PUBLIC SCHOOLS.

The public schools of this village are what are known as the "District Schools," each of the four wards of the village being a distinct district and having its separate schools and buildings.

These districts are comprised within, and compose a part of the district school system of the town of Watervliet, the system being first established and organized in 1813, and has continued ever since. The districts within this village are designated as follows: First ward, District No. 1; Second ward, District No. 2; Third ward, District No. 20; Fourth ward, District No. 9. At the time of the organization of these school districts, the school-house for District No. 1 was located at the village of Washington, afterward know as the village of Port Schuyler; the school-house for District No. 2 being located at the village of Gibbonsville; and the school-house for District No. 9 being located in the country. District No. 20 was not organized until some years afterward, and was created from a portion of District No. 2.

TURNPIKE AND PLANK ROADS.

The Troy and Schenectady Turnpike.—This turnpike road was incorporated in 1806, and in May of that year was surveyed and laid out by Lawrence Vrooman. The charter granted the construction of a road from Ferry street, Troy, to the village of Schenectady. This road was constructed and owned by a company composed of the principal merchants of the City of Troy, and was built for the purpose of diverting from the City of Albany the extensive grain traffic which it then had from Schenectady. This road ran through the land upon which this village now stands, and in laying out the village this road was called Genesee street within the village limits. The road was abandoned and surrendered to the town of Watervliet a number of years ago.

Watervliet Plank Road Company.—This company was incorporated and the road constructed in 1850, running from Buffalo street north through Broad street, now Broadway, in this village, to Auburn street, where it crossed over to the west side of the canal, and thence to the village of Cohoes. This road never paid any dividends to the stockholders, and after an existence of ten years was abandoned and the charter surrendered.

Broadway of this village was originally a post road or turnpike, and was known as the Whitehall Turnpike, also as the Northern Turnpike. Along this road from the City of Albany to Whitehall were placed mile-stones; the stone known as the seven-mile stone was located in this village, at a point a short distance south of Genesee street, this point being seven miles distant from State street, Albany.

OLD RESIDENTS.

Of the original settlers of this village, there are at present only three now living and residing in the village, namely: Messrs. Samuel S. Wandell, Henry Kimberly and Morgan L. Taylor.

Mr. Samuel S. Wandell came to this village (then Gibbonsville) to reside in 1828; previous to that date he had resided in the City of Troy, where he was born in the year 1800, at the home of his father, known as the Wandell homestead, which was located on the bank of the river near what is now known as Division street. Mr. Wandell is a painter by trade, and for more than 30 years previous to 1862 kept a store for the sale of paints, oils, etc., in this village, and also worked at his trade. Mr. Wandell is now the oldest person living that was born in the City of Troy.

Mr. Henry Kimberly was born in Troy, on February 20, 1806. He learned the trade of a blacksmith in the City of Albany, and in the spring of 1827 came to West Troy to reside, and opened a blacksmith shop, which was located on the southwest corner of Broadway and Ontario streets. At that time there were only three other buildings on Broadway; a large wooden building used as a store, on the southwest corner of Broadway and Union streets, which was conducted by the firm of Pattison & Hart; a small wooden dwelling a short distance south of this store, and an old tavern near the ferry.

Mr. Kimberly, by his industry, prudence and honesty, has become one of the largest real estate owners of this village. In 1836 he was elected a Trustee from the Third ward of this village, being

THE VILLAGE OF WEST TROY.

one of the first trustees after its incorporation in that year.

Mr. Morgan L. Taylor was born at Ballston, Saratoga County, May 18, 1806, and came to this village to reside in 1828; and for a greater part of the time that he has resided here his business interests have been closely connected with the canals and river. For a number of years previous to 1878 he and Hiram Holbrook, under the firm name of Holbrook & Taylor, owned and carried on the canal boat dry dock in this village, known as the West Troy Dry Dock, which is located at the southern terminus of Washington street. Mr. Taylor was elected to the office of President of this village in 1852, and held the same for the term of one year.

PUBLIC MEN.

Lorenzo D. Collins was elected Member of Assembly for the year 1859, and re-elected for 1860; and in November, 1865, was elected State Senator for the years 1866-7.

Waters W. Braman was elected Member of Assembly for the year 1874, and re-elected for 1875, and again elected for the year 1879; and in November, 1879, was elected State Senator for the years 1880-1.

Peter A. Rogers was elected Surrogate of Albany County in November, 1871, and entered upon the discharge of the duties of the office on January 1, 1872, and, at the expiration of his term of office, was re-elected and continued to the office until January 1, 1884.

POLICE.

The first police force in this village was organized, under an act of the Legislature, in 1865, and was known as the "Capital Police District." This district comprised the cities of Albany, Troy and Schenectady, the villages of West Troy, Green Island, Lansingburgh, Cohoes and Greenbush, and certain portions of the towns of Watervliet and North Greenbush. The district was divided into two divisions, known as the "Troy Division" and "Albany Division," this village being embraced within the Troy Division. The first Deputy Superintendent of the Troy Division was John M. Landon. The West Troy Precinct was located at 38 Broadway. The first officers and patrolmen were as follows: Captain, Lansing Clute; Sergeant, Abram E. Lansing; Patrolmen, C. Spencer Loomis, Richard Crooks, Martin V. B. Jones, James Smith, Charles H. Cary, John W. Decker and Patrick Rogers.

In 1870 the present police force of this village was organized by virtue of an act of the Legislature of that year; this act repealed the Capital Police District act or law, in so far as it related to this village, and gave the electors of this village power to elect four Police Commissioners, who had power to organize and maintain a police force in this village. The first Commissioners elected under this act were Ebenezer Scoville, John I. Winne, William C. Durant and Isaac R. Getty. These Commissioners in that year organized a police force, and appointed James O. Wood, Captain, and Sylvanus K. Jefferson, Sergeant, who have held the respective positions ever since such appointment.

CIVIL WAR.

Monday, July 1, 1861, was an eventful day in the history of this village, it being the day of the last visit of Co. A, 34th Regiment, New York State Volunteers, prior to their departure for the seat of war in the war of the late rebellion. This company was composed of volunteers who were residents of this village; the company being formed by the efforts of William L. Oswald, who was at this time president of this village. On this day the company came from the barracks at Albany, and were met at the train by the citizens and members of the fire department and escorted to the North Reformed Dutch Church, in front of which had been erected a large platform, over which hung a large American flag. The Rev. G. W. Hathaway, on behalf of the "Ladies' Volunteer Association," welcomed the company, and presented them with two large boxes of useful articles for camp and hospital use. The Rev. O. H. Gregory then addressed the soldiers, and, on behalf of the Watervliet Bible Society, presented each officer and private with a bible, upon the inside of the cover of which was fastened a slip which bore the United States flag and the words "To the Defenders of Our Country."

A beautiful national ensign, made of silk, a gift of the citizens of this village, was next presented to the company, George R. Meenely making the presentation address. After that the company made a short parade through the village and then took the train for the camp, many of the members never to see this village again. This company was composed of the following named citizens: Captain, William L. Oswald; Lieutenant, Elijah R. Brown; Ensign, Benjamin H. Warford; Orderly Sergeant, Luther A. Hill; Second Sergeant, George H. Swartwout; Third Sergeant, John Oothout; Fourth Sergeant, Martin Gorman; First Corporal, Abram E. Lansing; Second Corporal, John McIntyre; Third Corporal, Joseph Andrews; Fourth Corporal, Edward Hoffman; Henry L. Witbeck, Daniel Cassidy, Edgar Lorman, Thomas Cary, Henry Gilman, Alonzo Hills, James McCormick, Anthony Kelly, Daniel M. Becker, Louis Hoffman, John B. Amsden, James A. Britton, William Campbell, Robert H. Hartley, Richard Rapson, George Porter, Patrick Horan, Edward Donohue, Martin Troy, Thomas F. Colligan, Sidney Hockridge, Patrick Keenan, James Anderson, William Traver, Levi Colwell, Henry White, George Hecock, Martin Luckey, John Walsh, John Tottie, Edward Thompson, John Morey, James M. Shoemaker, William H. Bartlet, John Dailey, Riley C. Witmarsh, Spencer Hoffman, John Cunningham, Martin Buck, John Barnett, John McMullen, Peter Ost, James Dongan, Henry Lorman, Thomas Kelley, William J. Cary, Peter Van Patten, Jacob C. Forman, Charles Dorn, Alexander Hannah, John Dolan, Charles Mitchell, James P. Allen, James Redden, Charles Traver, David Flanagin, Frank Hayden, Albert W. Houce, John Loan, William Kirk, Henry W. Price,

Alphonzo Dubois, David Cary, James Donohue, Patrick Welsh. On the 2d day of July, this regiment, under Col. Ladue, left for the seat of war, embarking on the propeller *Henry Adams* and a barge from the city of Albany, the place of their encampment.

FIRE DEPARTMENT.

The present organized fire companies of the fire department of this village consist of four hose companies and one hook and ladder company. They are as follows: Oswald Hose Company No. 1, organized 1859; Michael Kelly Hose Company No. 2, organized 1870; Thomas McIntyre Hose Company No. 3, organized 1873; Protective Hose Company No. 4, organized 1878; S. J. Gleason Hook and Ladder Company No. 1, organized 1872. In 1864 the first steam fire engine of this fire department was purchased, and company organized and named James Roy No. 1. In 1867 another steamer was purchased and company organized and named James Duffy No. 2, and in 1873 another steamer was purchased and company organized and named Martin Tierney No. 3. These steamers remained in active service until 1878, when the system of public water works, at that time introduced into this village, was deemed sufficient to extinguish all ordinary fires, and the steamers stored for use in case of emergency, and the respective companies were disbanded.

The old fire department of this village of twenty-five years ago consisted of three hand-engines and two hook and ladder companies, and were as follows: Rip Van Winkle Engine Company No. 1, Protection Engine Company No. 2, and Conqueror Engine Company No. 3; Hercules Hook and Ladder Company No 1, and Spartan Hook and Ladder Company No. 2. All these old companies were disbanded twenty years or more ago, but at what dates it cannot be ascertained.

From the organization of this village until 1881 the control of the fire department was vested in the village Board of Trustees. In the last-mentioned year, by act of the Legislature, the control was taken from the trustees and vested in a Board of Fire Commissioners, which was created by said act, and who were to be appointed by the said village trustees.

RAILROAD.

The first steam railroad which ran through this village was constructed in 1852 by the Albany and Northern Railway Company (now leased and run by the Delaware and Hudson Canal Company). The builders of this railroad intended to construct the roadway through this village, along or near the bank of the Hudson River. To this the inhabitants strongly objected, as it would necessarily impair the value of the most valuable property of the village, besides greatly interfere with our most important business interests; consequently, the road was constructed through the extreme western part of the village, and a station located at Genesee street. This depot being so far from the central part of the village, Mr. Samuel Hill ran a stage for passengers from the West Troy Ferry, at the foot of Canal street, to the depot.

After a few years the railroad company decided to give better accommodations to the public, and therefore erected a small wooden depot on the north side of Canal street (now Central avenue), a short distance west of Erie street, the cars being backed down to the depot by means of a short track constructed through this street to the main track, and connected therewith by means of a switch, called a Y. This depot had a small bell hung in a tower upon the roof of the depot, which was rung when the trains were being "backed down" to the depot. For a number of years Mr. Lorenzo E. Abbott filled the position of ticket agent at this old depot.

In the fall of 1864 this depot and short branch track were abandoned, the location of the depot being transferred to the original location at Genesee street.

FRATERNAL SOCIETIES.

Evening Star Lodge (Masonic), No. 75.—The first Masonic lodge located in the town of Watervliet was known as Clinton Lodge, No. 202. The date of the charter of this lodge was December 12, 1811. It became inoperative somewhere about 1818.

A lodge known as Evening Star, No. 466, was organized in that part of this village which was called Gibbonsville, and a charter or warrant granted, June 10, 1826. The following named brethren were its first officers: Joseph Hayward, Master; Ira Holdridge, Senior Warden; Obediah D. Brown, Junior Warden. This lodge went out of existence, date unknown, and was revived by authority of the Grand Lodge on January 31, 1840, John D. Willard, Junior Grand Warden, installing its officers as follows: Jacob Gingrich, Master; Jonathan Hart, Senior Warden; Luther M. Tracy, Junior Warden; Wm. P. Lansing, Secretary; Jacob Clute, Treasurer. At this installation Mr. Joseph Hayward, its first Master, was present.

On the 4th of June, 1840, the Grand Lodge changed the "lodge number" of this lodge to 75. On April 12, 1854, this lodge surrendered its warrant, pursuant to a resolution adopted at a meeting held for that purpose, the brethren having been duly summoned. The officers at this time were as follows: Daniel E. Stewart, Master; George B. Frazer, Senior Warden; Lorenzo D. Collins, Junior Warden; John E. Glass, Secretary; Morgan L. Taylor, Treasurer; Wm. McClellan, Senior Deacon; John W. Fisher, Junior Deacon, and John Christie, Tyler.

The present organization of this lodge dates from March 4, 1864, at which time Grand Master Clinton F. Paige issued a dispensation to the brethren at West Troy to form a lodge, to be known as "Evening Star," and subsequently received a warrant, dated June 17, 1864. The following were its first officers: Daniel W. Talcott, Master; Wm. Andrews, Jr., Senior Warden; Geo. F. Milliman, Junior Warden; Alexander McAllister, Treasurer; John H. Fitchett, Secretary; R. G. Smith, Senior

THE VILLAGE OF WEST TROY.

Deacon; Charles H. Fort, Junior Deacon, and William Fox, Tyler.

The Grand Lodge in June, 1864, adopted the following resolution:

Resolved, That the Evening Star Lodge, U. D., be permitted to receive and work under the dormant warrant of a lodge once known as Evening Star Lodge, No. 75, and to be hereafter hailed and known as such number.

This lodge has been in successful operation since the date of its present organization, March 8, 1864. This lodge has been unfortunate, as in June, 1865, its lodge room, with all furniture and records, were destroyed by fire, and again, in December, 1870, its lodge room, together with all its elegant furniture, etc., met the same fate.

In connection with the Evening Star Lodge, in 1871, was organized a chapter of the Royal Arch Masons, known as Hudson River Chapter, No. 262, the first officers being as follows: Albert Tayer, High Priest; Alfred W. Richardson, King; Charles L. Mather, Scribe; Geo. B. Mosher, Treasurer, and Henry C. Kelsey, Secretary. This chapter is still in successful operation.

Laurel Lodge, No. 24, Independent Order of Odd Fellows.—This is the first regular lodge of this order organized in this village. This lodge was first organized and charter granted on January 21, 1846, and given the lodge number of " 209." The persons petitioning for the charter, and to whom the same was granted by the Grand Lodge, were as follows: Alexander S. Lobdell, L. D. Lawrence, Samuel Wilgus, James H. Marshall, E. F. Hitchcock, Stephen F. Washburn, George A. Shields, Joseph Schwikhardt, Lewis J. Williams, Robert Kilby, S. Greenman, Robert I. Moe, George B. Fraser, Isaac R. Getty, James E. Dorman, James Cook, Robert Robinson, E. I. Higgins and Ariel Wager.

When the State of New York was divided into two Grand Lodges, "Northern" and "Southern" New York, this lodge joined the Northern New York division, and was given No. 39 for its lodge number. In 1866, when the two jurisdictions came together, this lodge was given the number of " 24," which it now retains.

Although Laurel Lodge was the first regularly organized lodge in this village, yet in or about the year 1838 there was a lodge in this village which was called "Watervliet Lodge, No. 20," and held meetings at a private residence of one of the members, on Broadway, south of the United States Arsenal. This lodge was expelled by the Grand Lodge as illegally organized, not having received a charter from the same.

BANKS.

The first bank located in this village was organized and incorporated in 1836, and called the "Watervliet Bank." The officers were as follows: John C. Schuyler, Jr., President; Edward Learned, Vice-President; Egbert Olcott, Cashier; Gerrit T. Witbeek, Teller, and George M. Wheeler, Clerk; the capital stock being $100,000. The banking house was located in the brick dwelling house situated on the southwest corner of Broadway and Buffalo street. This bank failed in 1841.

" *The National Bank of West Troy.*"—This bank was first organized and incorporated, under the laws of this State, in February, 1852, and commenced business May 1, 1852, under the name of "Bank of West Troy;" the capital stock being $200,000, divided into 2,000 shares. John Knickerbacker, James Van Schoonhoven, James Roy, E. Thompson Gale, John Cramer, Joseph M. Haswell, William Sands, George H. Cramer and Ferdinand J. Suydam were the original incorporators and constituted the first board of directors; the officers being as follows: Ferdinand J. Suydam, President; George H. Cramer, Vice-President; Albert C. Gunnison, Cashier. In 1853 Ferdinand J. Suydam became Cashier, and Mr. G. B. Wilson became Discount Clerk and Bookkeeper. In 1858 Mr. Suydam resigned his position as cashier, and in May of that year Mr. G. B. Wilson became his successor and held the position for about nineteen years. In 1877 Mr. Benjamin McE. Schafer became cashier and held the position until his decease, in 1880, when his successor, the present incumbent, Mr. Arthur T. Phelps, was appointed.

In 1853 Mr. Dillon Beebe was elected president, and held the office until 1856, when Mr. Joseph M. Haswell became his successor. Mr. Haswell held this office until the date of his decease, in 1871.

Mr. James Roy was elected as the successor of Mr. Haswell and held the office until 1876, when Mr. Thomas A. Knickerbacker, the present president, was elected.

The banking house used by this bank, and situated on the southwest corner of Washington street and Central avenue, was erected in 1852, for the use and occupation of this bank, by Mr. Ebenezer Wiswall.

This bank was converted into a National Banking Association in 1865, and the name changed to the "National Bank of West Troy;" the capital stock being $250,000, divided into shares of $100 each. In 1877 the capital stock was reduced to $150,000, and in 1883 was still further reduced to $100,000, which is the amount of the present capital stock. On the 21st day of May, 1885, the corporate existence of this bank was extended until the close of business on the 24th day of May, 1905, by order of H. W. Cannon, Comptroller of U. S. Currency.

PUBLIC BUILDINGS.

Corporation Hall.—This is the only public building in this village. It is a three-story brick building, situate on the east side of Broadway, midway between Central avenue and Buffalo street, and was erected in 1864 by the village corporation at a cost of $20,000. The first and second stories are occupied by the Fire Department and meeting room of the Board of Fire Commissioners; the third story as a meeting room or council chamber for the Board of Village Trustees.

NEWSPAPERS.

The first newspaper of any importance published in this village was the *West Troy Advocate*, the first publication being in September, 1837. This paper was printed and published weekly by William Hollands, who continued its publication until his decease, in January, 1853, when his son, William Hollands, Jr., continued the publication until its discontinuance, in July, 1864. Mr. Hollands is now one of the leading lawyers of this village.

The next newspaper which was published in this village was a weekly, called the *Albany County Democrat*, which was first published in January, 1860, and was edited by Mr. Allen Corey, who continued to publish this paper until July, 1884, when he sold it to the publisher of the *Watervliet Journal*.

The next newspaper of any importance published in this village was a weekly, called the *Watervliet Journal*. This paper was first published by James Treanor in May, 1880, and continued until July 5, 1884, when Mr. Treanor purchased the *Albany County Democrat*, and merged these two papers into a paper called the *Journal and Democrat*, which is now published by the firm of Treanor & Hardin.

About the year 1832, there was published in West Troy a newspaper called the *Palladium*. This paper was edited and published by two young men, who were brothers, under the firm name of Warren Bros. In connection with their printing office they also kept a stationery and book store, which was located on the northeast corner of Canal street and Broadway, on the site now occupied by the Collins House.

SCHUYLER MANSION.

Located on the bank of the Hudson River, a few rods from the present southern limits of this village, stands the oldest building in this vicinity. This building is a brick structure, two stories, with high gable roof. It is now owned and occupied by Richard P. Schuyler, Esq., as his family residence, and is known as the "Old Schuyler Mansion." This building was erected about the year 1768, and was built to replace the original mansion that was, at about that date, destroyed by fire. It stands upon the foundation of the original mansion. The date of the erection of the original mansion is unknown, but it was probably erected some time previous to the year 1700.

In 1672, Philip Schuyler, the father of Col. Peter Schuyler, purchased a large tract of land from Kiliaen Van Rensselaer, which included the lands to the south of this village, and known as the "Flats," and also included the land upon which the southern portion of this village is located. The flats were occupied for agricultural purposes as early as 1642, as from that year until 1660 they were occupied by Arent Van Curler, and after him by Richard Van Rensselaer.

On September 14, 1691, Peter Schuyler, son of Philip Schuyler, and afterward known as Col. Peter Schuyler, married Maria Van Rensselaer, the sister of Kiliaen Van Rensselaer, the patroon; and in April, 1711, located his residence at the Flats, in the mansion; at this date and until about the year 1806 the main road from Albany ran along the bank of the river, and passed here between the mansion and the river. At about the date that Col. Peter Schuyler took up his residence at the Flats the public safety began to be greatly endangered by the insidious wiles of the French Canadians and the hostilities of the Indians, and the Colonel became a person of much importance by reason of his influence with the friendly Indians, he being their true friend and a person in whom they placed much confidence.

About the year 1708 it was thought advisable to send some of the chiefs of the friendly tribes to England upon a visit, so as to attach them to that country, and that they might see the sovereign of the English nation, and to counteract the false statements of the power and wealth of that nation which the French Canadians had been circulating among them; but it was no easy task to get them to consent to the proposal. At last, however, they consented, upon the condition only that Col. Peter Schuyler would accompany them, as he had never been known to tell a lie, or to speak without thinking. The Colonel consented, and the adventure succeeded beyond his expectations. The chiefs were much pleased with the attention shown them and with the kind and gracious manner of Queen Anne. She was also much pleased with the Colonel, and desired to knight him, but he respectfully and positively refused, stating as his reason that it would not be in keeping with the simple manners and habits of his life and surroundings. In 1719 Philip Schuyler, the eldest son of Col. Peter Schuyler, married Catalina Schuyler, his cousin, whose father had for a number of years been the Mayor of the City of Albany. Catalina was a person of superior character, and was known during the latter part of her life as "Madame Schuyler."

Philip, at the decease of his father, became the owner of the Flats and mansion, and became a person of great importance in the public affairs of the country, being a member of the Colonial Assembly, also a Colonel, and being the first person who raised a corps in the interior of the province of New York, which fought in the French and Indian War.

Col. Philip died in February, 1758, and was survived by widow, the "Madame," and, as he left no children, he devised his property to his widow during her life, and thereafter to his great-nephew, Peter Schuyler, who was at that time an orphan, and resided with him. The remains of Col. Philip were interred in the family burying-ground, which is located a short distance from the mansion, and over the grave is erected a handsome monument, which still remains as placed there in 1758. This old mansion has always remained in the Schuyler family and been occupied by the descendants of the original owner, Philip Schuyler.

WEST TROY GAS LIGHT COMPANY.

The West Troy Gas Light Company was incorporated in January, 1853, under the provisions of

THE VILLAGE OF WEST TROY.

the general act of the Legislature for the formation of gas light companies. The original incorporators were: Richard S. Lobdell, A. V. Barringer, Morgan L. Taylor, Albert Richards and E. H. St. John; the capital stock being $100,000.

Previous to the date of the incorporation of this company, and in October, 1852, John Lockwood and A. V. Barringer, under the firm name of Jno. Lockwood & Co., obtained the exclusive privilege, from the president and trustees of this village, to lay gas mains through the streets and alleys of this village, and to erect and maintain gas works, etc.; and in November, 1853, John Lockwood and A. V. Barringer assigned their rights and privileges to the West Troy Gas Light Company. In July, 1853, this company obtained from the president and trustees of the village of Green Island the exclusive right and privilege of laying pipes through the streets of said village, and supplying it with illuminating gas. On the first day of February, 1853, this company elected Albert Richards, President; Morgan L. Taylor, Secretary, and Richard S. Lobdell, Treasurer.

On April 1, 1854, Wm. L. Oswald was appointed superintendent of this company, and continued to hold this position until the spring of 1862. In June, 1862, Edwin A. Smith was appointed superintendent, and held the position until the fall of 1864, when he was succeeded by Richard S. Lobdell. Mr. Lobdell held the position until March, 1879, when he was succeeded by the present superintendent, Richard F. Hall. Mr. Albert Richards remained the president of this company from the date of its organization to 1866, when he was succeeded by James Roy, who held the office until 1876, when he was succeeded by E. Thompson Gale, of Troy, N. Y. In March, 1879, the present president, George W. Chapman, succeeded Mr. Gale. In 1876 the manufacturing of gas by this company was discontinued, the company taking its supply of gas from the People's Gas Light Company, of Albany; but this did not prove a success, and, in 1879, this company commenced to manufacture gas at their own works, which are located on the northwest corner of West and Geneva streets in this village.

WATER WORKS COMPANY.

The West Troy Water Works Company was incorporated in 1876, under the provisions of the general act of the Legislature of this State, of 1873, for the formation and incorporation of water works companies, the water being introduced into the village in the early part of 1877. The first Board of Directors of this company were as follows: George R. Meneely, Alfred Mosher, George M. Wiswall, Jesse C. Dayton, Lorenzo D. Collins, John Reiley, George Tweddle, William B. Williams, Richard S. Lobdell and George B. Mosher. The water supplied by this company is obtained from the Mohawk River, at a point near Niskayuna, and is carried from this point, where it is pumped from the river, to a large storage reservoir located on the hill, about a mile west of the U. S. Arsenal, from whence it flows into the mains which run through the streets of this village. In 1877 this company introduced the water into the village of Green Island by extending their mains through the village streets. The expense or cost of construction of this system of water works was about $275,000, the village of Green Island being supplied with twenty hydrants and this village with ninety hydrants, which are used for extinguishing fires by the village fire department. This company has in use about sixteen miles of pipe, and supplies the water to consumers at a pressure of about seventy pounds to the square inch.

MANUFACTORIES AND BUSINESS ESTABLISHMENTS.

The mills which are located in the southern part of the village, and commonly called the Roy Mills, were established by Mr. James Roy about the year 1847. These mills are two separate establishments, one being conducted by the firm of James Roy & Co., and the other by the firm of Roy & Co., James Roy & Co. being engaged in the manufacture of shawls and woolen cloth suitable for clothing for men and women. Roy & Co. are engaged in the manufacture of butts, hinges and several other articles of builders' hardware, which are made from iron, steel and brass. The firm of James Roy & Co. in 1870 became a corporation, pursuant to the laws of this State, and took the name of "Messrs. James Roy & Co," the capital stock being $500,000, and the incorporators and trustees being James Roy, Benjamin Knower, John Knower and John F. Roy. This manufactory has three mills, two located at this village and one at Schenectady, N. Y., and gives employment to 700 operatives, and produces annually manufactured goods to the value of $800,000. These mills are also called "Watervliet Mills." The firm of Roy & Co. also became a corporation in 1871, under the name of "Roy & Co.," with a capital stock of $150,000, the incorporators and trustees being James Roy, John Knower and Peter Roy. This manufactory has an annual production of about $350,000 worth of manufactured stock, and employs about 350 operatives.

The founder of these large manufactories, Mr. James Roy, was a native of Scotland, and was born near Sterling. He learned the trade or art of a brewer of beer, and came to America in 1835, and was employed in a brewery at Pittsfield, Mass., and in a few years afterward came to this village and became the manager in the brewery of Archibald Dunlop, which was then located on the northwest corner of Spring street and Broadway; and while in the employ of Mr. Dunlop, Mr. Roy, together with Mr. John Knower, became the proprietors of the woolen mill and commenced the manufacture of woolen shawls, they sending to Scotland for a number of their employees that had been employed in the shawl factories in that country. Mr. Roy resided in this village and did much for its welfare and growth, and after a life of much usefulness, died at his residence in 1878, being survived by three daughters: Anna, wife of Capt. A. H. Sweny; Mary, wife of Capt. G. A. Sweny; and Alice, an unmarried daughter. Mr. Roy's only

HISTORY OF THE COUNTY OF ALBANY.

son, James, was accidentally drowned at Richfield Springs in 1869, aged 23 years.

The Meneely Bell Foundry was established in 1826 by Andrew Meneely, upon the present location of this foundry. Mr. Meneely learned the trade of a brass founder and mathematical instrument maker of Mr. Julius Hanks, who kept a small shop or foundry, which was then located on the west side of Broadway, about one hundred feet south of Buffalo street, in what was then called the village of Gibbonsville. Mr. Meneely commenced business as a manufacturer of civil engineering instruments, and also the manufacturing of church bells and town clocks. This business steadily increased, and in 1835 he took Jonas V. Oothout into partnership with him, the firm name being Meneely & Oothout. This firm continued to exist until 1841, when Mr. Oothout withdrew, and Mr. Meneely continued the business alone until 1849, when he took his son Edwin A. in the business as a partner, the firm name being Andrew Meneely & Son. In 1851 Andrew Meneely died, and this business was thereafter conducted by his two sons, Edwin A. and George R., under the firm name of Andrew Meneely's Sons; and a few years thereafter changed to E. A. & G. R. Meneely. Soon after the decease of Mr. Andrew Meneely, his successors discontinued the manufacture of civil engineering instruments (Mr. Meneely having discontinued the manufacture of town clocks previous to his decease), and gave their exclusive attention to the manufacture of church bells and chimes of bells, fire-alarm bells, etc. In 1874 Mr. George R. Meneely withdrew from this business, and thereafter the present firm name of Meneely & Co. was adopted, the present members of the firm being Edwin A. Meneely and his sons, Andrew H. and George K. This foundry has a world-wide reputation, having for many years sent bells of its manufacture to all parts of the world. The proprietors of this foundry have from time to time made several improvements in the form of the bells and the manner of hanging them, so as to make the labor of ringing as easy as possible.

FACTORIES.

The Brass Foundry of George R. Meneely & Co. was established in 1874 by Mr. George R. Meneely, for the manufacture of a patent journal bearing for steam cars, locomotives, etc. This firm has another foundry, which is located at Atlanta, Ga., where the same patent bearing is manufactured. The firm carries on an extensive business, supplying most of the principal railroads with journals of their manufacture.

The Meneely Hardware Company is a private manufacturing corporation, which was incorporated in 1882, the incorporators and trustees being George R. Meneely, Charles D. Meneely and John Gibbons, the wares manufactured by this company being harness, rope and chain snaps, also rope goods for horses and cattle, many of the wares being the inventions of Mr. John Gibbons above mentioned.

The Covert Manufacturing Company was organized in the City of Troy, N. Y., in 1873, the original members of the firm being James C. Covert, Madison Covert, Henry Wakeman and Scudder Wakeman. In 1879 this establishment removed from Troy to this village, and soon afterward the Messrs. Wakeman withdrew from the firm, leaving the Messrs. Covert the sole proprietors.

The goods originally manufactured by this firm were harness snaps, rope goods and saddlery, hardware specialties. In 1883 the Messrs. Covert added to the manufacture of the class of goods above mentioned the extensive manufacture of all kinds of wrought iron chains, from the lightest to the heaviest grades.

POTTERY.

The manufactory of earthenware, commonly called "The Pottery," which he located on the southwest corner of Washington and Schenectady streets, was established in 1831 by Mr. Sanford S. Perry, the factory at that date being located on Champlain street, fronting the Erie Canal, a short distance above Buffalo street. This pottery was purchased of Mr. Perry in 1845 by the firm of Porter & Fraser (Nathan Porter and Robert H. Fraser), and by this firm in that year removed to its present location. About a year afterward Mr. Fraser died, and his brother, George B. Fraser, succeeded him as a member of the firm. This firm continued for eighteen years, when it was dissolved, each of the members retiring from active business, and the pottery and business being sold to Mr. George H. Seymour, of Troy, N. Y., and thereafter conducted by him, and now conducted by the firm of Shepley & Smiths.

Mr. Nathan Porter, who is now one of our oldest citizens, was born in Brookfield, Mass., in 1809, and came to this village to reside in 1839.

Mr. George B. Fraser was born at Athens, N. Y., and came to this village in 1845, and remained a resident until his decease in 1884, aged 78 years.

JONES' CAR WORKS.

J. M. Jones' Sons Horse-Car Works was first established as a manufactory of wagons and carriages in 1839 by Messrs. Henry W. Witbeck and John M. Jones, under the firm name of Witbeck & Jones. This firm continued to manufacture wagons and carriages until 1863, when Mr. Witbeck withdrew from the business and Mr. George Lawrence took his place; and upon the advent of Mr. Lawrence, the firm's attention was first directed to the building of horse-cars in connection with their regular business, and the manufacture of wagons and carriages was soon afterward abandoned for the manufacture of horse-cars only. In 1864 Mr. Lawrence was obliged to withdraw from the business on account of ill health, Mr. Jones purchasing his interest and associating his sons in the business with him, under the firm name of J. M. Jones & Co. In February, 1882, Mr. John M. Jones died, and his sons, John H. and Walter A., continued the business, under the firm name of J. M. Jones' Sons.

The cars manufactured by this firm have world-wide reputation. Cars of its manufacture are now being used in South America, East Indies and other foreign countries, besides in all parts of the United States and Canadas.

In January, 1879, these works were removed to Schenectady, but remained there only for a short time, having returned to West Troy in 1883. Mr. John A. O'Haire, the superintendent of these works, has been continuously employed there since 1854. Mr. Robert Waugh, the superintendent of the painting department, has been an employee of these works for more than forty years.

PLANING AND SAWING MILLS.

The James Kerslake Planing, Sawing and Molding Mill was originally erected by Mr. Kilgour in 1852, and he was succeeded by Messrs. Ufford & Latham, and Mr. Kerslake succeeded Messrs. Ufford & Latham in 1873, becoming the sole owner of the entire mill property. Mr. Kerslake continued to conduct this mill until his decease, July 9, 1882, and since that date the business has been carried on by his widow. The entire establishment is in charge of and under the control of Mr. Waters W. Braman, the general manager.

The Rousseau & Harrington Planing Mill was established by Mr. Lewis Rousseau, the senior member of this firm, in 1834, and he thereupon entered into copartnership with Mr. Easton, the firm name being Rousseau & Easton. This copartnership continued for twenty-eight years, when Mr. Easton withdrew from the business. Mr. Rousseau always remained interested in this business since its establishment. The present junior member of this firm, Mr. Arvin W. Harrington, is a son-in-law of Mr. Rousseau. Mr. Rousseau was born in Troy, September 24, 1804, and lived there for the first thirty years of his life, when he removed to this village in 1834. He was also the founder of the Watervliet Bible Society.

Mr. Rousseau died very suddenly, at this village, on July 2, 1884.

The Dry Goods and Wall Paper establishment of James D. Lobdell's Sons was established by James D. Lobdell in 1847, and he continued to carry on the business until his decease, January 18, 1879, when his sons, Messrs. William, Edward and James, succeeded to the business, and carried on the same under the above mentioned firm name.

On February 1, 1884, Mr. James Lobdell withdrew from the firm, and the business is now carried on by Messrs. William and Edward Lobdell under the same firm name.

In 1829 Mr. James Lobdell, the grandfather of the present proprietors of this establishment, opened a dry goods store in West Troy, and ever since that date the Lobdells have conducted the principal dry goods establishments of this village.

HISTORY OF THE TOWNSHIP OF WATERVLIET.

By JACOB S. MARKLE.

INTRODUCTION.

THE pages devoted to the history of Watervliet have been gathered and carefully written from sources that were attainable, and from information kindly given by those who had knowledge of the facts, events or circumstances connected in some way with the several subjects under consideration, and from which important data was obtainable. Old deeds and other records have been of much value, and from these information of general interest has been freely given. Personal assistance was rendered in some instances, for which the writer acknowledges his indebtedness and kindly returns his sincere thanks.

The limit of the work precludes much that might be introduced, did it not trespass upon the general plan of the history and conflict with the province of other writers.

We have thus imperfectly traced the records and historical associations connected with the changes and modern progress of this old township, from its early settlement in colonial times, and its struggles, to its present modest prosperity; and much of this has something to remind us of the stalwart patriotism of its founders and the enthusiasm which belongs to a people of intelligence, physical vigor and exalted manhood.

ALBANY, 1885.

WATERVLIET TOWNSHIP.

The Manor of Rensselaerwyck was erected into a district, March 24, 1772, and subdivided into East and West districts, March 5, 1779, the river being the separating line. The West District, as defined by act of March, 1772, embraced all that part of the manor north of an east and west line from Beeren Island north to Cumberland County, except the City of Albany.

The name of WATERVLIET is of Dutch origin, from *water* and *vlakte*, level plains or flats. The level lands or flats along the river were and are subject to overflow in time of freshets; hence they are the "*overflowed flats*" or *water-vlakte*, the last word corrupted into "*vliet*," which is incorrect, as *vliet* in the Dutch language means *river*.

This township was the first one organized in the county, and was formed, March 7, 1788, and included the West District of the Manor of Rensselaerwyck, with Colonial or State lands on the north. That part of the city north of Patroon and Quackenbos streets, known as the *Colonie*, was incorporated, March 31, 1791, and again, March 30, 1801. April 9, 1804,* it was made a village, and April 11, 1808, it was organized by the Legislature as a township, in which it continued to exercise civil and political privileges until February 25, 1815, when the township was divided, a part merged into the bounds of the City of Albany and the remaining portion reannexed to Watervliet. In 1870 a part of this old *Colonie* was taken from Watervliet and annexed to Albany City.

The township has undergone many changes since its formation in 1788, when it included all the territory as now represented by the several townships, Cohoes and Niskayuna. The following changes have taken place and other divisions formed from this parent since its organization:

Rensselaerville was taken off in 1790, Coeymans in 1791, Bethlehem in 1793, Guilderland in 1803, Niskayuna in 1809; a part of Colonie was annexed in 1815; Cohoes was taken off in 1869, and in 1870 a portion was annexed to Albany City. West Troy and Green Island, parts of the township, are incorporated villages.

The township is triangular in shape, resting upon one point, and occupies the northeast corner in the county.

It is bounded on the north by Schenectady and Saratoga Counties, on the east by Saratoga and Rensselaer Counties, on the south by Rensselaer

---

* The following, from the session laws of 1804, reads: "An act to vest certain powers in the freeholders and inhabitants of that part of the Town of Water Vliet, in the County of Albany, commonly called the Colonie, which was incorporated, April 9, 1804, as follows: 'Lying on the west bank of Hudson's River, in the northeast bounds of the City of Albany; extending north about three-fourths of a mile to Mill Creek; thence west one mile up along the said creek; thence southerly with a line parallel to the said river till it strikes the north bounds of said city; thence east to the place of beginning.'" The village was to elect five persons as trustees, who were empowered to make by-laws, levy taxes and perform other duties; a Treasurer, Collector and five Assessors were also to be elected by the freeholders. The first town meeting was held at the house of William Kane, in April, 1809, no records of which can be found.

County, Albany City and Guilderland, and on the west by Albany and Guilderland. The Hudson and Mohawk Rivers flow along the east and north boundary, separating it from Rensselaer and Saratoga Counties.

The number of acres of land assessed in 1883 was 33,560; the assessed and equalized valuation of personal and real estate for 1883 was $5,524,828.97; the assessed valuation of West Troy and Green Island, $4,875,076.21; total for the township, $10,399,904.18. Population in 1865, 27,275; 1870, 22,609; 1875, 20,894; 1880, 22,220. The surface is broken into plains and uplands, which have an elevation of from 200 to 300 feet. The declivities of this upland have numerous gullies, worn by the small streams, while the Mohawk on the east has made precipitous banks and deep cuttings above and below the falls; swamps and small marshes are numerous. A fine interval of alluvial soil, varying in width, extends along the Hudson; this is frequently overflowed by freshets, and the deposit which accumulates renders the soil very fertile. The soil along the river flats is a rich alluvium, and a light sandy loam upon the upland and plains. There are mild sulphur and chalybeate springs. Bog iron ore is found in a few locations, and some graywacke quarries furnish excellent building and flagging stone.

The streams or creeks are small. The principal ones are Patroon's Creek, with its tributaries, Sand Kill, Lisha's or Lychus Kill, Town Branch, Schauline Creek, Donker Kill, Dry Branch, Ralger Kill and Red Creek. The acreage of woodland is rapidly diminishing, and only small patches remain, containing a few acres, and small groves preserved for ornament or wind-breaks. Roads and turnpikes are numerous, and are kept in good traveling condition, and railroads traverse through the town in many directions.

The first settlements in this township were made upon lands included in the Van Rensselaer Manor. The great inducement and favorable terms upon which settlers could obtain these lands were at that time of much importance and advantage to them in their condition. Their means were very limited, and their wealth consisted mostly of their families, a few necessary supplies and hardy constitutions. The wilderness which surrounded them could be made to bear fruit, and after many days of toil and hardship, struggling against poverty and self-denial, they saw the result of their labor, performed with rude implements, in fair crops of grain and forage, an increase in live stock, more acres ready for cultivation, and some of the comforts of life to be enjoyed in old age. But the course of prosperity does not always run without friction; disturbing elements cannot always be guarded against; conflicts at that time were of varying kinds, and these often interfered with the lone settler's security and domestic comfort.

In time civilization threw her protecting arms about them, thus securing their lives and property from savage and wanton destruction; society made advances; moral progress was strengthened into spiritual life, and knowledge was nurtured in the school of adversity. It was this robust and pioneer experience that gave action and power to a class of men who accepted the conditions necessary to educate them for citizens, asserting their self-reliance and principles of individual right in the affairs of popular government and the relations of social progress. These early colonists exhibited shrewdness in the selection of their lands for farming purposes, and in locating their future homes near the settlement in the colony of Rensselaerwyck, so that they were under the protection of Fort Orange in time of trouble, and could enjoy other privileges with those at the fort. Albany at that time was an outpost of civilization, around which clustered a community of Dutch, who were engaged in the fur trade with the Mohawks and other tribes of Indians. They were a rude and not always overscrupulous people, were anxious to accumulate wealth, and ready for the best bargain, that they might add to their possessions, and share in the enviable honors, however won, of their neighbors.

The Hollanders were wise in gaining the friendship of the Indians, thus securing a measure of safety from their stealthy, savage raids, at the same time the better to control the trade in furs with them; yet they were unwise in introducing disturbing elements in the civilization of these savages—the use of the tomahawk and rifle, and the greater evil, firewater. This sudden change was so great that the Indian added to his own bad habits many of those of the white man, thus developing all his inherent savageness and brutal tortures, to be used against those who brought not the best, but a destructive, agent in civilization.

The first settlements in what is now Watervliet were made north of the city, along the river, extending to Port Schuyler, now a part of West Troy. The Van Rensselaers occupied most of the land in the vicinity of the Colonie; then came the Schuylers and a few other families whose interests and business were more directly connected with Albany. From a map of the Van Renselaer Manor, made in 1767, there were then but 148 families west of the Hudson River. The following names are given as settlers at that time in what is now Watervliet. Those along the Hudson from Albany to the mouth of the Mohawk were : Jeremiah Schuyler, Peter Schuyler, Col. Philip Schuyler, Peter Cluet (west of the Schuylers), Jonas Sharp, Guy Young, Hans Van Arnum, Jan Outhout, Henry Bullsing, Cornelius Van Denbergh, Wirt Van Denbergh. Along the Mohawk from its mouth north : Jonas Outhout, Abram Van Denbergh, Cornelius Van Denbergh *alias* King, —— Lansing, Henry Lansing, Cornelius Onderkerk, Douw Fonday, Franz Lansing, Dirk Hemstraet; and at the Boght: Hans Lansing, William Liverse, Jan Douwe Fonda (Frederick Clute and —— Wynans on colonial lands). Along the Mohawk, west of the Boght: Daniel Van Olinda, Jacob Clute, Bastian Visher, Jacob Freltie, Diederick Scheffer, Martys Bovee, Fransway Bovie, Hans Heemstraet, Bastian Cregier, —— Duyvepagh, Simon Groet, Hans Cluet, Robert Canier. In the northwest corner: —— Consaloe, Hans Consaloe, Isaac Truax; and the following who lived over the manor line, —— Cluet, John Schuyler, Nicholas Hallenbeck and Glen Braat. On the sand road to Schenectady, John Richies, at the Knil; Christie, at the Sandbergh, and a family at the Verfbergh.

Many of these early settlers have left their names and descendants to perpetuate some quality of their ancestry; and whether the scene be laid in the primitive forest, or upon the cultivated field, the same struggles brought out invigorating elements of character, which were qualities essential to their robust manhood, which gave them an influence in civil affairs, and communicated spiritual life to the rude state of society. Many others have departed with no record by which to follow their outgoings, and their names are lost for all time. Others came and took their places as actors in the great problem of human liberty to be solved by persistent exertion. From a record in the possession of Peter Lansing, of Lishaskill, the history and genealogy of Hendrick Lansing is taken, Peter being a lineal descendant and representative of this family, whose great-grandfather settled in Watervliet about 1700.

Hendrick Lansing, of the town of Hasselt, in the province of Overyssel, was the ancestor of all the Lansings in America. His son Gerret early came to Beaverwyck from Hasselt, near Swoll Overyssel, and died before October, 1679. His sons were Hendrick, Gerrit and Johannes, and from these have originated the several families. The daughters were Hilletie, who married Storm Van Derzee, son of Albert Andriesen Bradt, and their daughter Anne married Johannes Becker; Alltie married Gerrit Van Slichtenhorst; Gysbertie married Hendrick Janse Roseboom.

Hendrick Lansing, son of Gerrit, was in Albany as early as 1666, and died July, 1709. His son Jacob married Hellina Pruyn, and their son Hendrick J. married Lena Winne, 1769. Hellina died in 1827. Jacob died in 1792. Their son Benjamin married Mary Tymerson. Their children were: Peter, who married Catharine Norris; Helen, who married Lewis Morris; Henry B., who married Eliza Putnam, and afterward Sarah Knight; Cornelius T., who married, first, Catharine Billson, then Caroline Steers. This family settled at Lisha's Kill, and comprise one branch of the Lansings.

Col. John V. A. Lansing, who married Harriet Verplank, came here in 1791 or 1792, and settled on the farm where his grandson, Vischer Lansing, lives. He had four sons and four daughters. The four brothers married sisters, daughters of Cornelius Groat; Abram V. P. Lansing married Helen Groat; Gulian V. P. Lansing married Catharine; Jacob J. married Rachael, and John married Eliza.

The daughters of John V. A. married as follows: Maria, first, Richard J. Pearse, then Garret L. Winne ; Williamke, Sebastian Pearse ; Helen, Jacob Weaver, and Harriet, Jacob C. Lansing.

From this family have originated the following professional men: Rev. Dr. John A. Lansing, Revs. Abram G. Lansing, Gulian Lansing and his son John G., Jacob Pearse, Nicholas Pearse and Augustus Pearse, Elmer C. Lansing and J. McCarrol Lansing, physicians; Howard Lansing and Christopher Lansing, attorneys at law.

Two brothers, Gerret and Ryckert-Claas Van Vranken, sons of Claas Van Vranken, early bought lands in Niskayuna. From these descended the families of this name in that town. Gerrit, son of Claas, married Ariantje Uldrick, and their children were Claas Uldrick, born 1685, and Maritie, born 1690. Claas in 1704 married Geertruy Quackenbos; their son Petrus married Neeltie, daughter of Dirk Groat, and from this family are the descendants of Watervliet, and the Groats are probably descended from this family and from Seymun Groat.

Jacob Lansing and his wife, Hellena Huyck, came from Holland at an early date, about 1700, and his son John settled in the vicinity of the Boght, on the farm now owned by Egbert Lansing. Rutger Lansing's son Gerret settled on the Mo-

HISTORY OF THE COUNTY OF ALBANY.

hawk, above the falls, and here are the possessions and improvements of Isaac D. F. Lansing, extending along the river, and at the Aqueduct. In 1795 J. D. F. Lansing built a large two-storied brick dwelling house, near the Cohoes dam, which is still standing and occupied. Teunis Lansing's family are represented by the children of Francis T.

Daniel Van Olinda was an early resident, and obtained a certain piece of land from John De Puyster, which is described in a deed of sale, given to Isaac Fonda, July, 1738. Portions of this property remain in the possession of his descendants.

Isaac Fonda was from Holland, and born in 1715, and in 1749 married Cornelia De Friest, and his line of descent to the present time is through his son Isaac I., then Isaac I., Jr., Cornelius I., James V. V., Daniel D. and Charles Fonda. When Isaac Fonda obtained possession of this property the following persons were on adjoining lands: Gerardus Kloett, Hendrick Rider, Jacob Lansing, Dirk Bradt.

Mr. James V. V. Fonda (son of Cornelius I.), 80 years old, is living on the original homestead, and part of the old house, built before the revolution, is attached to a dwelling near the road, and in this small room Richard Kloet kept a tavern during the stormy days of revolutionary times, when Indians and Tories gave the neighbors much trouble, for here they would meet and discuss the stirring events of the day, which were generally boisterous after the firewater began to burn. Tradition repeats the story that Gen. Washington at one time was a guest in this house, and stood upon the same floor now in use, and that an Indian, who became angered, threw a tomahawk at Dick Kloet, but, missing him, struck a beam, the mark of which is now concealed by repairs. Also, that Gen. Morgan and his soldiers camped and occupied the hill near the canal, and quartered his men upon the families in the vicinity. This seems to be historical ground. Mr. Fonda, who relates the above and many other incidents, has in his possession a Holland Bible, printed in 1713; also, a powder horn, with the name James Bouyngy engraved upon it, with the date 1756, and other designs. He has also an old sword, inscribed with date of 1758, with the initials P. D. Another curiosity is an "*Ulster County Gazette,*" published at Kingston, January 4, 1800, by Samuel Freer & Son, containing a full account of the death of Washington, with letters from England and France, and address of John Adams, and proceedings of Congress.

Douw Fonda and wife were from Holland, and his family was perpetuated by the descendants of his two sons, Abram and Douw. Other families of Fondas were Isaac H. and Henry I., the name being numerous in the township.

The Van Rensselaer patent did not include the whole of Watervliet, the northeastern portion being government land, and deeds were given by England, as the one here mentioned, now in the possession of Lansing Van Denbergh, who kindly permits a record of it to be taken. It is written on parchment, in large English script, has no signature, but a great seal of the crown, three inches in diameter, half inch thick, of wax, and now broken in many pieces. It is dated October 21, 1697.

"William the Third, by the grace of God, King of England, Scotland and France and Ireland and Zealand, and Defender of the Faith, greeting: Our loyal subject, Peter Hendrich De Haas: All that land between the Cohoos and Conn-Hagioewa, on the south side of Schinictady River, lying between the two Creeks, about two miles in length, more or less; in breadth from east side of a marsh, including the said marsh, &c., &c., at an annual rental of twenty shillings, &c."

This tract of land came into the possession of Peter P. and Gerrit P., sons of Peter Van Denbergh. In 1805 a partition deed was given by Peter P. to the sons of Peter P., viz.: Douw, Peter G., Isaac G. and Cornelius G. Van Denbergh.

This property was in the vicinity of the Boght, and some portions remain in the family.

Another family of early settlers was Jacob Cluet and his sons, Johannes J. and Jacob. This family owned a farm north of Town-house Corners, and Luykes Witbeck received a deed of this property from Stephen Van Rensselaer, dated February 27, 1769, in the ninth year of the reign of George III.

Luykes Witbeck had three sons, Abram L., Gerret and John, and from these brothers the name descended to the several families of Watervliet. John L., son of Lucas I., and grandson of John, lives upon the original farm. The above deed is witnessed by Lucas Van Vechten, Nicholas Cluet and Cornelius Wendell. Mr. John L. Witbeck has in his possession a small brass brasier, which is old and rare, from the Fonda family; also, a remarkable piece of embroidery upon silk.

At the commencement of hostilities with England, the inhabitants of this town were included in the west district of the manor of Rensselaerwyck, and many of them held lands leased by the patroon at an annual rental. Farms, at first, were located in the vicinity of Fort Orange, for protec-

THE TOWNSHIP OF WATERVLIET.

tion. The settlements gradually extended beyond, and finally occupied the level lands along the Hudson and Mohawk Rivers. One of the most important considerations of the founders of this colony was to secure the trade in furs with the Indians, and to do this the Indians were induced to bring their peltries to Fort Orange for exchange. At certain periods of the year they came down the Mohawk to Schenectady or the falls in canoes, and then by trails to the place of barter. These trails or paths were afterward used by the whites as roads, of which three at least diverged from Albany—one leading direct to Schenectady, with a branch to the west; another across the center of the town to the Mohawk, and one along the Hudson up to the bend or boght of the Mohawk.

With few exceptions the first settlers were Dutch, and they readily conformed to all the laws and requirements as promulgated by those in authority. A peaceable yet persistent people, with simple habits of living, industrious and persevering, strongly attached to early traditions of justice and religion, they planted upon this soil principles and practices which were the underlying source of success, and the issues that followed were the result of loyalty and patriotism.

In carefully studying the condition of the people as well as that of the country, the observer will at once notice the wonderful change that was wrought when hostilities ceased, and peace once more smiled upon a nation, now free and independent. Every condition of prosperity, every branch of industry, every public or private enterprise, manufactures, agriculture, commerce, churches, schools and professions were now open and ready for development. All seemed to spring into new life with an impulse that was irresistible, and the spirit of progress swept with renewed force over the land, of which this district received a large share.

At this time, about 1785, the way is open for a new element to mingle with Holland society, and many families from New England and the adjacent counties improved the opportunity and located among the Dutch, occupying lands under leases from the patroon. This immigration, in their intercourse and association in the affairs of government, politics, religion and education, introduced the ideas and principles of Puritanism which they received as a legacy from the New England teachers, and these were advanced and instilled into the minds of the people, and a unity of sentiment in essential things was in time accepted, the results of which have been a blessing to the community in elevating morality.

Since 1800 the advantages derived from an intelligent and liberal course of education, as well as popular government, have been seconded by the rapid advancement of general literature and aided by the newspaper, in the cultivation of knowledge which enlarges the mind and fosters a spirit of investigation for higher culture in the natural and general sciences, the laws of mechanics and industrial pursuits.

These have been well received in the town, as its general prosperity attests. The internal improvements, its numerous manufactures, its public and private enterprises, its mechanical pursuits, its rapid advance in agriculture, its system of modern schools and institutions of practical sciences, its freedom of religious sentiment as proclaimed from the numerous churches and religious societies, denote the progress and enlightenment of the people, and the prosperity of those who contributed to the general welfare. The rural portion of the town has an industrious population engaged in that occupation that forms the basis of every nation's prosperity, the tillage of the soil.

Of late years the methods of farming have been based upon practical systems, and the advancement in special agricultural knowledge from scientific investigation and practical experiments. These are sources from which the intelligent farmer will obtain suggestions and results of much value, and the careful study of agricultural journals is of more value to the farmer than the purely political newspaper.

Improved machinery and labor-saving implements are the farmer's greatest boon; these, with judicious breeding of live stock, are a source of wealth to the intelligent farmer who exercises wisdom and prudence in all things pertaining to rural economy. A large part of the cultivated acres in the township is devoted to dairy purposes, for the production of milk to supply the demands of Albany, Cohoes, West Troy, Green Island and the neighboring villages. Mixed gardening—vegetables and small fruits—is an industry of considerable magnitude, extensively conducted upon small farms by Germans and others.

Below is given a list of supervisors, justices of the peace and town clerks from 1793 to 1844. The first town meeting of which there is any record was held at the house of Isaac Truax, Jr., on the 2d day of April, 1793. The figures denote the year when the person was elected.

Supervisors: Stephen Van Rensselaer, 1793; Jacob Winne, 1795; Cornelius Glen, 1801; Enoch Leonard, 1804; Stephen Van Rensselaer,

1808; John Schuyler, Jr., 1810; Lucas G. Witbeck, 1824; Francis Lansing, 1827; John C. Schuyler, 1833; Jeremiah Schuyler, 1837; Gilbert I. Van Zandt, 1838 to 1851.

Justices of the Peace (by appointment)—Jurian Hogan, 1797; Jedidiah Strong, 1809; H. V. Cuyler, 1809; Nicholas Freligh, 1810; Stephen M. Conger, 1811; Lyman Stanford, 1811; Jedidiah Baker, 1817; E. Wilson, Jr., Jacob I. Wager, 1820. Special town meeting, December 22, 1822, the following were elected: Jedidiah Strong, Philip Lennenbacker, Elijah Ranney, Stephen M. Conger, Daniel Van Dyke, 1827; Isaac Fonda, Jr., 1827; Ethical Enders, Isaac H. Williams and Frederic V. Waterman, 1831; A.

W. Richardson, 1833; Stephen Groesbeck and Lawrence V. K. Van Demark, 1834; Francis O. Dorr and Jonathan Kash, 1836; John Hastings, 1838; Supply F. Wilson and William King, 1839; Jonathan Hart, 1840; Martin Winne, 1841; Matthew Fort, 1842; James M. Barnard, 1844.

Town Clerks—Luther Trowbridge, 1793; Gerret Clute, 1800; Benjamin Winne, 1802; Levinus L. Winne, 1805; Harmanus V. Cuyler, 1809; Lyman Swan, 1811; John G. Ruby, 1813; Gerret T. Lansing, 1826; Stephen Groesbeck, 1833; Martin Witbeck, 1834; William R. Peake, 1835; Oliver Burr, 1838; John Mason, 1842; Cole H. Denio, 1843; Robert I. Moe, 1844.

NEW YORK STATE SURVEY.—PRELIMINARY GEOGRAPHICAL POSITION OF STATIONS AND MONUMENTS IN WATERVLIET.

NAME OF STATION.	NO. OF MONUMENT.	OWNER'S NAME.	LATITUDE.			LONGITUDE.		
Arsenal	237	U. S. Government	42°	43'	09"	73°	42'	07"
Center Street	240	On Green Island	42°	44'	33"	73°	41'	27"
Lansing Pine	15	Benjamin Lansing	42°	45'	37"	73°	50'	38"
Race Course	236	Erastus Corning	42°	41'	16"	73°	42'	55"
Lishaskill P. O., Reformed Church	....		42°	45'	20"	73°	52'	36"
N. Y. C. R. R. Shops, Tall Chimney	....	West Albany	42°	40'	38"	73°	46'	30"
Williams Monument in Rural Cemetery	....		42°	41'	53"	73°	44'	16"
County Line Monument	43	Watervliet & Niskayuna	42°	46'	43"	73°	47'	59"
" " "	97	Watervliet & Niskayuna In road opposite T. J. Miller's store.	42°	46'	19"	73°	49'	26"

Nestigione Patent, in Saratoga County, and Connestigione, another old patent, granted in 1697 to Peter Hendrix De Haas, are the origin of Niskayuna, and of an extensive tract on both sides of the Mohawk. The latter was west of the Cohoes Falls and within the present township of Watervliet. The Erie Canal enters this town from Saratoga County in the northeast corner, crossing the Mohawk at the lower aqueduct, and winds along the margin of that river, by the Cohoes Falls and through the city of Cohoes; thence southerly and forms a junction with the Champlain Canal, just above West Troy, through which it passes, across the Arsenal grounds, and thence along the Hudson River flats through North Albany—the great lumber market—and by the Van Rensselaer mansion, to the Albany basin, about 13 miles in this town, having 19 locks, 165 feet descent, and two locks of 22 feet descent at the side just opposite Troy.

West Albany R. R. Y. M. C. A.—In March, 1876, Mr. E. D. Ingersol, general railroad secretary of the Y. M. C. A. of America, called a meeting for the purpose of organizing an association, which was held in the machine shops of the New York Central and Hudson River Railroad at West Albany, which resulted in the election of Mr. T. F. Blackburn as president. George S. Spencer became the first general secretary in October, 1876. Present membership, 193.

The following have served as presidents since Mr. Blackburn: Walter Van Guysling, William F. Horth, Seth Clark, Charles A. McBain, W. H. Rockenstive, Oliver S. Vedder, E. W. Morgan, and L. Packard, the present incumbent. The secretaries have been George S. Spencer, George M. Heckendon, Augustus C. Doerscher and E. W. Gorton.

VILLAGES, POST-OFFICES AND HAMLETS.

Boght (or Groesbeck's Corners), an old-settled place in the northeast corner of the township, in the bend or boght of the Mohawk, on the Loudonville road, and near Crescent station, west of Cohoes, contains twenty dwellings, Reformed Church, parsonage, school-house No. 18, shoe shop, and formerly a store. This vicinity and the Aqueduct were settled by Van Denberghs, Van

De Marks, Fondas, Clutes, Van Vrankens, Lansings, and later by Wm. Groesbeck, the Simons, Godfreys, Roffs, Dunsbacks, and Runkels.

North of the Boght is the Aqueduct, containing dry-dock and brick-yards, and north is Dunsback Ferry, across the Mohawk. Here John Van De Mark kept tavern, and early settlers were Van Vrankens. The Erie Canal crosses the Mohawk River in the northeast corner by a stone aqueduct, $1,137\frac{1}{2}$ feet long, resting on 26 piers, which are 26 feet high, and contains 18 locks.

Town House Corners (Van Vranken's, and now Latham's Corners), is a hamlet at the crossing of the Loudonville road and the Troy and Schenectady turnpike, six miles from Albany. Has been known by the above names from local causes. The neighborhood was settled by Van Den Berghs, Witbecks, Van Olindas, Van Vrankens, Oothouts and Mathias Markle. Joseph Yearsley and Myndert Van Denbergh kept taverns many years ago. The neighborhood is thickly settled and contains 41 dwellings, Reformed Church, parsonage, school-house No. 11, hotel, James Latham, proprietor, and blacksmith shop. Dr. Jonas Wade located in the vicinity as early as 1806; was a successful practitioner in his day, and much reputed for his many good qualities. His son, E. M. Wade, succeeds him, and another son, Edward Wade, is a lawyer of Albany City.

Watervliet Center (P. O.) is a small hamlet in the northern central part of the township, located on the Troy and Schenectady turnpike, two miles north of the Shaker settlement, and contains thirty-six dwellings, two stores, James Pearse, merchant and postmaster; William Graham & Brother, general merchandise; Abram W. Fraleigh, proprietor of the hotel; two blacksmith shops and wheelwright shop. School-house No. 6, built as early as 1800, and the old house in which Laban Hills kept tavern in 1820, are landmarks.

The postmasters have been Laban Hills, Lewis Morris, and James Pearse, the present incumbent.

Early settlers in the vicinity were Witbecks, Orlops, Van Vrankens, Groats, Feros, Dr. Fraley, Sickles and Forts, at Fort's Ferry. Those who came after were Chamberlain, Gallager, Weatherwax, Cragiers and Lewis Morris, who came about 1835, and made great improvements in erecting hotel, store and several shops of which he was proprietor, and from this circumstance the place is known as Morrisville.

Near here, on the Town Creek, were the mills and woolen factories of Henry Waterbury, and on the same creek near Fort's Ferry were the Shaker mills.

Shaker's (P. O.), two miles south of Watervliet Center, and eight miles north of Albany, is the settlement now comprising the four families of the Shakers who located here in 1775, on lands leased from the Patroon, then a wilderness. The settlement number's 300 souls. This is a favorite resort for visitors in summer, and is reached by a pleasant drive on the Shaker road. For full details see County History.

Lisha's Kill (P. O.), name derived from an Indian who is said to be buried on the bank of the creek near Visher Lansing's, is a small hamlet in the northwest corner of the town, on the old Albany and Schenectady turnpike, nine miles northwest from Albany, and near the Central Railroad.

The first settler was Jacob Lansing, grandfather of Benjamin, and his descendants are numerous in the vicinity. Another early settler was John V. A. Lansing, who came in 1792. Many of his descendants are residents of the neighborhood. These were followed by Van Benthuysens, Ostroms, Van Zandts, Groats, Bulsons, Campbells, Stanfords. Charles Stanford kept a tavern on the turnpike as early as 1803. He was an enterprising and respected citizen, and was the father of ex-Governor Stanford. Here for many years was C. Lansing's tavern and Morris' store. The post-office was established about 1830. Postmasters have been Lewis and Jacob Morris. Peter Lansing was appointed in 1848, and is the present incumbent. Mr. Lansing is also proprietor of a general merchandise store, notary public, and formerly kept a hotel. The neighborhood is thickly settled with thrifty farmers. Two school houses, Nos. 7 and 8, afford the children facilities for education. The Reformed Church, parsonage and sheds attached, are conveniences for spiritual instruction, and comforts for the farmers' horses. A blacksmith shop near by is a necessity, and the toll-gate is a relic of former days, when six-horse teams, with heavy freight wagons loaded with merchandise, were passing and repassing at all hours of the day.

Newtonville (P.O.), formerly Newton's Corners—names given in honor of John M. Newton, who came here about 1840, and soon after erected a dwelling, and in 1850 a building for a store. He was an enterprising citizen and deservedly respected. He was engaged in active business during his life, and his sons continue the same line of business in the city where they reside.

The post-office was established in 1850. John Holmes was the first postmaster, and retains the office up to this time. President Arthur's father was Holmes' bondsman.

This hamlet is on each side of the Loudon road, four miles north of Albany, and is pleasantly located. Has a Methodist church and parsonage, school-house No. 13, store, of which John H. Kemp is proprietor, in which the post-office is kept. Here are located the shops of James Brewster, for the manufacture and sale of wagons, carriages and sleighs and general jobbing work; located at Ireland's Corners in 1851; came here in 1876 as James Brewster & Son; the firm is now James Brewster's Sons (James C. and William H.). The original Methodist church was built about two miles from here, near Lawson's, and for several years a boarding school—"Home Lawn"—was conducted by the Cole family. Rev. William Arthur (father of President Arthur), a Baptist preacher, also was principal of a private school for some time. The Baptist church (now abandoned) is just on the borders of the village. Early residents in the vicinity were Gilbert Waterman, Capt. Van Olinda, John Gornay and others. Dr. H. C. Abrams is located here as physician. Following the plank road south, on either side, are many fine residences and farm houses, which continue for the intervening short distance, and Ireland's Corners (P. O.), now Loudonville (P. O.), is reached. This is a thriving and lovely suburban hamlet, three miles from Albany, on the Loudonville plank road. The name is from Lord Loudon, and the road was in use previous to and during the revolutionary war.

The village owes its first name to Elias H. Ireland, who bought the lands in 1832 of Van Rensselaer, then all woods and only three houses or families near him. Jonathan Seeley Ireland was a preacher in the early days of Methodism, and being independent, he was his own sexton. Thomas Seeley Ireland, father of Elias, had settled in the vicinity previously, as well as Charles T. Ireland and John Ruby. Dr. Peter B. Noxen came here soon after E. H. Ireland, and practiced medicine during his lifetime. He was located at first at Coeymans Landing. Elias made improvements, engaged in the hotel and merchandise business, was quite successful, and died in 1870. His property has changed hands and great improvements are being made. The post-office was established about 1850, Elias H. Ireland, postmaster ; name changed to Loudonville, 1871 ; Samuel Bacon, postmaster. James Brewster located here in 1851, for the manufacture and sale of wagons, carriages and sleighs; in 1876 he removed to Newtonville.

There is a store, containing general merchandise, in which is kept the post-office, Ralph H. Gove, proprietor, also present postmaster. School-house No. 11 is pleasantly located and arranged for two teachers.

This is the finest and most desirable suburb of Albany, and with Newtonville, is a closely populated district. The Loudon plank road offers easy access and delightful drives. The surroundings possess many attractions, and as a quiet, rural resort, or place of residence, many of the business men of the city have fine mansions, beautiful lawns, gardens and green-houses, which are much admired for their cheerful and home attractions. These, with the surroundings of the neighborhood and the natural scenery quite diversified, possess many striking features. Among those who reside here, and have done so much for the permanent benefit and encouragement of a higher order and cultivation of the beautiful in nature and art, are Samuel Bacon, P. K. Diedrick, George L. Steadman and John C. Hughson.

Center Station, in the western part of the town, on the Central Railroad, is a collection of a few houses, and the place is a way-station, which furnishes conveniences to the residents of the neighborhood.

Menand's Station, on the Albany and Northern Railroad, is the location of Louis Menand's extensive green-houses, flower gardens and nursery grounds, which were established by the present proprietor in 1842. Here are located the fair grounds, originally intended for the use of the State Agricultural Society.

They contain several buildings, sheds and ample accommodation for poultry, live stock, manufactures, machinery, domestic and agricultural products and implements. The place is convenient of access from all points by steamboats, railroads and horse cars. The State Fair for the present year, 1885, is appointed to be held here. The property is now owned by John Sundergan. Here also are located the Rural, St. Agnes and Anshe Emeth cemeteries.

Early settlers here were Schuylers, Ten Eycks, Gorways, Glens, Jermains, Hillhouse. The vicinity is now thickly populated, and many business men of Albany have their residences here. The attractions of natural scenery and the result of modern science and skill have changed the aspect of these low, hilly ridges and rendered them conspicuous and beautiful for situation, possessing many striking features for the skill of the artist to develop in design of architecture and landscape ornamentation.

West Albany P. O. (formerly Spencerville). This is a busy and thriving place, lying north of Pa-

THE TOWNSHIP OF WATERVLIET.

troon's Creek and west of the city line, two and a half miles from the City Hall, reached by State street and Central avenue horse cars, and New York Central Railroad cars, which pass through it. Here are located the extensive repair, machine and car shops, engine houses, cattle yards and other industries connected with the above railroad. The necessary ground occupied for the transaction, transfer and other purposes of the company's immense business at this place covers many acres; 1,500 men are employed, under competent superintendents and skilled foremen.

The stock yards here are next in importance to those of Chicago and Buffalo, and in former years the transaction in live stock was even more extensive.

The business was originally commenced as early as 1847, by Wm. Wolford and Gallup, on Washington avenue, afterward at the old "Bull's Head," on the Troy road, and then transferred to what is now the end of Central avenue by Hunter and Gallup. About 1860 the business was removed to its present location in West Albany, where large sheds and commodious buildings were erected, with other accommodations for feeding, transfer and shipment of stock.

For several years Allerton, Dutcher & Moore were proprietors of the cattle yards, and in November, 1868, Eastman Brothers became proprietors, and have continued to the present. They purchase 500,000 tons of hay for feeding the stock for one year. A large brick hotel, conducted by John Williamson, is located in the immediate vicinity of the yards, which furnishes accommodations for buyers and sellers.

The post-office was established, September, 1862, by the appointment of Joseph Mather postmaster. The present postmaster is George W. Gibbons. The business transacted here has materially fallen off for the past few years, which is attributed to the shipment of slaughtered beef, in refrigerator cars, to all the great cities, as well as live stock to foreign markets. The receipts of hogs and sheep do not show much change. The following table gives some important figures, which are obtained from reliable sources, and give the number of car loads for the years designated:

Year.	Car Loads Cattle.	Car Loads Sheep.	Car Loads Hogs.	Car Loads Horses.
1878.......	28,238	10,262	4,894	627
1879.......	31,484	9,923	5,449	949
1880.......	34,718	10,312	5,234	1,058
1881.......	33,452	10,057	5,153	906
1882.......	24,208	9,497	6,172	788
1883.......	20,847	10,718	6,595	717
1884.......	17,444	9,925	10,891	851

The following gives the number of live animals:

Year.	Car Loads Cattle.	Car Loads Sheep.	Car Loads Hogs.	Car Loads Horses.
1880.......	525,228	1,089,800	992,309	15,184
1881.......	568,225	1,608,120	979,070	11,778
1882.......	411,536	1,324,530	1,110,960	10,244
1883.......	375,200	1,690,650	961,300	8,808
1884.......	299,760	1,207,975	1,999,070	13,158

For the week ending December 31, 1884, there was received: Cattle, car loads, 3,910; sheep, car loads, 12,760; hogs, car loads, 25,500; horses, 80.

MANUFACTURES, MILLS AND OTHER INDUSTRIES.

Grist and saw-mills were erected on the small streams at an early date. These creeks furnished a limited water power, which served the people in their needs of lumber, flour and manufacture of domestic supplies. Remains of these early mills are in a few localities; others have been erected upon their ruins, thus have served their purpose, and now, with the strides of modern progress and invention, changes have been wrought, improvements made, and steam, in a great measure, monopolizes as a motive power the ancient water wheel.

Caldwell, Frazier & Co. had a factory, and —— Muir clothing works on Mill Creek as early as 1803. The Shakers had a grist and saw-mill about the same time. The Lansings had a saw-mill on Lisha's Creek. Grist and saw-mills have been operated for many years on the Schaline or Town Creek, near where it empties into the Mohawk. These are now operated by Taylor Brothers. A woolen factory, near Watervliet Center, on the same creek, was formerly conducted by the Waterburys. Mills and manufactories of various kinds were early erected and operated on the Patroon's Creek, in Tivoli Valley. These are now within the city boundary. With few exceptions, the mills, manufactories and industries are confined to the cities and villages.

The works of greatest magnitude now in the rural portion of the town are the fine brick buildings erected by Truman G. Younglove in 1866 as a straw-board paper mill, the lime and cement kilns and the Lansing grist-mill. These are located just below the "Cohoes Company's" dam, and near the Cohoes city line.

The paper mill has all the modern machinery and first-class fixtures; was operated by the owner and builder for three years; then passed into the "Cohoes Straw-Board Company," composed of T. G. Younglove & Co. (G. H. Stewart and Levi Dodge), who operated it till April 1, 1883. The property is now owned by Thomas Brisline. When in operation, seven tons of straw were manufactured into five tons of paper per day, requiring four tons of coal, and about twenty-eight men were employed. The monthly pay-roll amounted to $1,100. The motive power, turbine wheels, driven by water from the Cohoes Company's Canal.

The lime and cement works were started in 1869, by the "Capitol Lime and Cement Company," composed of Truman G. Younglove, George Stewart and David T. Lamb, of Waterford, and Henry Dunsback, of Crescent, Saratoga County. The kilns are not used at present. The mill is now operated for grinding soap-stone and marble. The property is now owned by Lewis Hoffman.

Here also is located the grist-mill which was originally owned by Gerret Lansing, and then by I. D. F. Lansing. Connected with it is the dwelling house erected in 1795. The work of greatest importance at this place is the dam across the Mohawk, above the falls, which furnishes the water power for the Cohoes industries.

The "Cohoes Company" was incorporated, March 28, 1826, with a capital of $250,000, which was increased, April 26, 1843, to $500,000. The first trustees of this company were Charles E. Dudley, Peter Remsen, Francis Olmstead, Stephen Van Rensselaer, Jr., Canvass White, David Wilkinson and Henry J. Wycoff. A dam was built across the river in 1831, which was carried away in 1832. Another was constructed, and this was partially destroyed in 1839, and rebuilt the same year. The company now own the entire water power from half a mile above to one mile below the falls, which gives a total descent of 120 feet.

The present stone dam was constructed in 1865, and is one of the most substantial and costly structures of the kind in the United States. The entire length of the dam is 1,443 feet, and with the head-gate and gate-house, which is of solid stone and brick masonry, built in 1866, cost $180,000.

The directors at this time were Alfred Wild, president; William T. Garner, Charles Van Benthuysen, David J. Johnson, Samuel W. Johnson, William W. Niles, and Truman G. Younglove, agent. The work was done under the supervision of the agent. The engineer was William E. Worden; assistant, David H. Van Auken; and contractor, John Bridgford.

Five canals at different levels are constructed, and the water is again used from the level of the State dam. These canals were constructed at different periods, the first in 1834, three-fourths of a mile long, with a fall of 18 feet; the second in 1845, one-third of a mile in length and a fall of 25 feet; the third is half a mile long and 23 feet fall. This and the previous one are parts of the old Erie Canal. The fourth and fifth have a fall of 20 feet each. The entire water power is estimated at 10,000 horse power, and all is not utilized. The abuttal of this dam on the east is the town of Waterford.

Henry O. Lansing, about 1875, built a custom grist and saw-mill on the Lisha's Kill, to be operated by water or steam, containing two run of stone and a corn-crusher; frame building. The Shakers have one of the largest saw mills in the town. There is not the demand for mills of this kind that there was formerly. As the forests are growing less, and timber is becoming scarce and increasing in value, farmers purchase their lumber and save their small forests.

CHURCH HISTORY AND SOCIETIES— WATERVLIET.

In collecting the history of the several church and religious organizations of Watervliet, the same conditions exist that prevailed with early organizations throughout the county. For many years the Reformed Dutch Church was the only organized religious body. The first pastor was Rev. Johannes Megapolensis, who came to Albany in 1642. The services were conducted in the Holland language for 140 years, and for seventy-five years this was the religion of this colony. At this time, 1716, the first Episcopal church west of the Hudson was opened for worship, and the Presbyterian church in 1761 or 1762, and it is well to know upon what authority the people were guaranteed the right of worship. Here is the foundation stone, contained in the "New York Charter of Liberties," upon which is built the fundamental principle of our government, and which should be sacredly held as a divine legacy:

"No person professing faith in God by Jesus Christ shall at any time be in any ways disquieted or questioned for any difference of opinion." The company was bound to give them local government; officers were to be appointed by the directors and council, and were invested with the religious privileges, as the following extract: "No other religion was to be publicly tolerated, save that taught and exercised by the authority of the Reformed Church in the United Provinces." This provision was imperfectly complied with, yet in 1639 "the Bible was declared to be the Constitution" by the government of the colony of New Haven. Then membership in the churches was largely under the control of the ministers, and civil and religious obedience was exacted from all. The Holland and English colonists had contended for religious liberty and vested rights, and they thought these could be best preserved by the protection of freedom in religious liberty and a conservative government which would secure equal political rights, to be adjusted by the people. To the early principles taught by these true men, in a spirit of intensified conscience that were destined to perform an important part in the civilization of this new world, are we largely indebted for this spirit of freedom and action, which is an inheritance to be preserved for all time as priceless.

It may be well to ascertain what were some of the causes that operated against the early formation of church societies disconnected and remote from those at Albany.

First, the country was slow of settlement and families were widely separated. Secondly, the wealth of these pioneers consisted in their poverty, hardships, self-denial, and in their rude cabins. Thirdly, the disturbed and unsettled condition of their surroundings rendered life and property unsafe, subject at any time to the attack of their cruel and savage enemies, the Indians.

As settlement advanced in the manor, material progress followed. This gave encouragement for renewed effort in the direction of religious privileges,

THE TOWNSHIP OF WATERVLIET.

which had in a great measure been denied them. As their means were yet limited, they collected or gathered in small bands at the most central house of a neighbor for private worship, and thus extended their religious views and influence among their immediate neighbors, and formed a nucleus for future growth. The first organized church or society beyond the city seems to have been in the town of Berne, about the year 1763, and one in Niskayuna, about the same time, both Reformed Dutch churches. The exact date of the organization of these churches with some others, is uncertain, as the records have been lost, and tradition is not always reliable. From this time no further efforts were made for the establishment of church organizations until after hostilities ceased and peace followed the war for independence, which at once opened the way for religious liberty and freedom to all classes and creeds.

It was from the Holland ancestors, who had fled from enforced cruelty and persecution, that these great principles of human liberty and conservative religious freedom were inherited ; yet we should not forget that spirit and system of moral development which was brought and fostered by the English, and particularly those who came from New England, who had also been tried by the same severe test of persecution, and which serves as a balance to preserve the forces which exalt religious freedom and energies, the rights of justice to the common interests of humanity. Moral progress and religious development which was now influenced by the revival or introduction of new elements, by the free expression of ideas and newspaper exhibits of intelligent views, brought a conflict of opinions and religious convictions that opened a spirit of discussion, and introduced practices somewhat unexpected in their results. Yet the test of vital piety and truth of the doctrines were practically sustained, and Calvanism maintained a place among the churches ; for at that time the Calvanistic faith and doctrines were attacked by other orthodox followers.

The lessons taught from this controversy were not without their powerful influence upon the revival of a purer Christianity, and the spirit of intolerance was in a measure swept away for the more charitable one of brotherly love.

The organization of Reformed churches in Watervliet was previous to its formation as a township; other denominations in time followed, and now there are three Reformed, three Methodist Episcopal, Presbyterian, one Roman Catholic. The churches of West Troy and Green Island are not included in the history of the rural district of Watervliet. The Boght Reformed (Dutch) Church is located in the northeast part of the town, above the Falls, and northwest of Cohoes, in the bend or elbow of the Mohawk River, boght being the Dutch for bend. For many years the nearest church was at Albany ; but they had worship among themselves, and a building was erected for occasional worship at an early period. There is no record of the first house of worship that was standing when the church was organized.

A petition, signed by forty-two persons, was presented to the Classis of Albany, February 22, 1784, and the first record of organization is April 14, 1784. From the relation afterward sustained between this church and the one at Niskayuna, it is evident that the Boght Church is to be regarded as the offspring of the Niskayuna congregation. As the Niskayuna Church was originally in Watervliet, some mention of it must form part of the history of this township. The precise date of its organization cannot be determined, as the facts and records, for the most part, have been lost. It appears, however, from the best sources of information to be obtained, that it was as early as 1760. After the organization of the church at the Boght, these two congregations were under one pastorate. The Rev. E. Westerlo, of Albany, for some time had the supervision of this church. The first pastor was the Rev. John Demarest, who began his ministry in 1790, taking charge of the Boght church in connection with the church of Niskayuna. He preached in the Dutch language, and records during his ministry are written in Dutch. He closed his ministry in 1803, and the union of the church of Niskayuna with the church of the Boght ceased at this time. In 1805 Rev. Dr. John Bassett was called, and continued pastor until the spring of 1811. During Dr. Bassett's pastorate services began to be in the English language, and stoves were introduced.

In 1806 the erection of a new church building was proposed, and Abram Witbeck, Douw H. Fonda and Dirk Clute were appointed a committee, and, after some discussion, the church was erected in 1807. The building was 40 x 50 feet, located on a pleasant spot, with a pine grove near it, on the road which is now the western limit of the city of Cohoes.

Rev. Robert Bronk became pastor in 1814, and also ministered to the church of Washington and Gibbonsville. He resigned his charge in 1823, having been pastor nine years.

June 28, 1824, a call was given to Rev. John B. Steele, and in February, 1833, he was dismissed, having been pastor nine years.

In 1825 it was ordered that D. A. Fonda and Martin Van Olinda conduct the singing, and that the precentors should stand before the pulpit.

Rev. Cornelius Bogardus was called as pastor, July 6, 1833, and he remained until 1838, about five years.

Rev. William Pitcher was called, January 13, 1840, and during his ministry it was proposed to build a new church, and, after full discussion and several meetings, the present building was erected, in 1847. This ground had been given for a parsonage nearly a hundred years previous. The land on which the parsonage stands was a part of the old De Haas patent, now known as the Van Denberg patent. Eight acres were given to the church, and the old Patroon of Albany afterward gave twenty-five acres upon the south side of the Manor line. That land was sold some years ago. There are about the present parsonage relics of the old parsonage which was built a hundred years ago. When the new church was about to be erected at the Boght, in 1847, a disagreement among the members as to the site resulted in the dismissal of twenty-two, who were organized as the Church of Rensselaer, and in the same year erected a church building in the south part of the congregation, at Van Vranken's Corners.

Mr. Pitcher's pastorate closed in 1854, after fourteen years of service. Rev. John Dubois was called in 1857, and continued pastor until 1859.

In 1860 Rev. John W. Major became pastor. He resigned in ill health, 1864, and died soon afterward.

In March, 1864, this church united with the church of Rensselaer in calling a pastor, and on the 20th of June Rev. Henry A. Raymond was called, who continued until 1871, when he resigned, and the following year the church was supplied by the Rev. C. P. Evans. The Rev. George I. Taylor was called, October 29, 1873, and began his services in the Boght and Rensselaer churches, January 1, 1874, and is the present pastor, having served ten years. Anniversary exercises commemorating the centennial of this church were held in the afternoon and evening, April 14, 1884. The church for the occasion was beautifully decorated with floral designs, an old Dutch Bible, and on one of the side walls was the old Dutch motto, *"Eendracht maakt macht,"* "Unity makes might." The exercises were varied, and were made doubly interesting by the many ministers who contributed their valuable services. The centennial sermon and discourse were delivered by the pastor, Rev. George I. Taylor, to whom the writer is indebted for much of the history of this church, taken by permission from the author's sermon, which was kindly furnished.

The first consistory of the Boght Church was: Elders, David Fero, Isaac Fonda. Deacons, Abram A. Fonda, Gerret I. Lansing. The present officers are: Elders, Jacob L. Van Denbergh, James H. Van Vranken, Benjamin Reamer. Deacons, Jesse A. Fonda, Nicholas I. Clute, Henry W. Fellows. The names of those who constituted the original church are appended, as showing who were residents of this neighborhood at that time: Francis Lansing. Gerrit, Evart, Mans, Wynant, Peter, Petras, Cornelius C., Cornelius 3d and Nicholas C. Van Denbergh, Gerrit Wendell, Luycas Witbeck, Jacob Van Olinda, Johannes Lansing, Rutgers Lansing, Johannes Clute, Isaac Fonda, Isaac H. Fonda, Timothy Hutton, Henry Fero, Christian Fero, David Fero, Jacob I. Lansing, Dirck Heemstraat, Charles Heemstraat, Isaac Onderkerk, Andrew Onderkerk, Johannes Fonda, Gerrit Clute, Isaac J. Fonda, Francis Cramer, Hendrick Wendell, Abram A. Fonda, Noah Gillet, Gerrit I. Lansing, Abraham H. Lansing, Jacob Lansing, Dirck Clute, Hendrick Fonda, Jacob D. Fonda, Abraham L. Witbeck, Abraham Onderkerk.

Ministers—Revs. John Demarest, 1790 to 1805; John Bassett, D. D., 1805–11; Robert Bronk, 1814–23; John B. Steele, 1824–33; Cornelius Bogardus, 1833–38; William Pitcher, 1840–54; John Dubois, 1854–59; John W. Major, 1860–64; Henry A. Raymond, 1864–71; George I. Taylor, 1874, present pastor, who reports 24 families, 35 members, 55 Sunday-school scholars, 6 teachers; contributions for the past year, $500.

The first officers of the Rensselaer Church were: Elders—Martin Van Olinda, E. J. Lansing, A. W. Van Denbergh. Deacons—Obadiah Van Denbergh, Nicholas V. V. Van Denbergh, Henry Van Alstine. Present elder, Jacob Osterhout. This congregation is composed of 12 families, the same number of communicants; Sunday-school scholars, 40; teachers, 7; contributions $500.

The Reformed Church of Lisha's Kill has no long history. The people of this neighborhood attended the old Niskayuna Church for Sabbath services until the second year of Rev. Goyn Talmage's ministry, 1852. At that time the church building at Niskayuna needed extensive repairs, and the ways and means were discussed, in which the people of Lisha's Kill did not give assent, but concluded to establish a church for their better accommodation at Lisha's Kill. This view was encouraged by Rev. Mr. Talmage and other leading men who moved in its favor. Application was made to the Classis of Schenectady by forty-eight members of the church of Niskayuna to be organized into a Reformed Dutch Church of Lisha's Kill. This application was made November 16, 1852, and was granted. The meeting for the organization was held in the upper school-house, district No. 8, Watervliet, December 5, 1852, at which time the organization was effected and the following persons were elected and ordained the consistory: Elders—Abraham V. P. Lansing and Jeremiah B. Ketchum; Deacons—Joseph Consaul and Cornelius Lansing. The church membership at this time consisted of forty-nine members. The next year, 1853, a church building of brick was erected, and dedicated March 30, 1854. In 1859 the parsonage was built, and in 1868 fifteen feet were added in length, and six feet additional for the pulpit recess; the whole interior was remodeled and refurnished, and dedicated March 18, 1869.

The pastors have been Rev. Goyn Talmage as a supply. Rev. Cornelius L. Wells was called in the summer of 1855, and after serving the church faithfully for two and a half years resigned in the spring of 1858. Rev. John A. DeBaun succeeded Mr. Wells in October, 1858, and continued pastor of this church and Niskayuna for 14 years; resigned his charge to accept a call from the church of Fonda.

The present pastor, Rev. Edward A. McCullum, was called to succeed Mr. DeBaun in 1883. The pastor reports 92 families, 154 communicants, 210 Sunday school scholars, 22 teachers, C. A. Lansing, superintendent. Total amount contributed for church purposes, $1,200. The church edifice is brick, with basement, has parsonage, and sheds for teams, will seat 300, and estimated value, $8,000.

The present officers, 1884, are: Elders—Charles Stanford, Cornelius A. Lansing, Abram G. Lansing, Simeon Fairlee. Deacons—George Stanford, Andrew Keenholtz, Jacob Spoore and Henry Lansing.

The above history of Lisha's Kill Reformed Church is largely compiled from an historical sermon by the Rev. John A. DeBaun, D. D., written in 1876, and kindly loaned by Daniel D. Ostrom, to whom thanks are due.

In the year 1859-60 John M. Newton, an enterprising citizen and resident of Newtonville, donated a lot of land, upon which was erected a church building of brick, for the use of a Baptist society. R. M. Pease was engaged in missionary efforts here, which was the origin of the Baptist organization. Other ministers who served as pastors of this congregation were Rev. John Reynolds, Rev. Dr. B. T. Welch, who died here, and his remains are in Albany Rural Cemetery, and Rev. William Arthur, father of Chester A. Arthur, late President of the United States. The society has been abandoned since 1869, and the property passed from the society by sale.

Other religious societies in the town are a Congregational Church, on the Shaker road, also a Methodist Church, on the Albany and Schenectady turnpike, south of Lisha's Kill, a Presbyterian Church and society on the same road, north of West Albany, and a Roman Catholic Church, at West Albany, erected in 1884.

The first records of the Congregational Society and Church of Watervliet, are dated in May, 1859, and the trustees were: Van Buren Lockrow, President; John Frost, Peter Steers, James Cramer, Daniel P. Sigourney and Henry Woolley, Secretary, Rev. James G. Cordell, Pastor. The church building was burned on the night of May 25, 1865. It was rebuilt the same year, and on December 20, at a meeting held in the school-room of the church, a motion was made by William Grounds and seconded by Norman Dings, "that the society assume the name of the Presbyterian Society of Pine Grove," while was unanimously carried.

February 5, 1867, this church and congregation were accepted by the Presbytery of Albany, and named the "Pine Grove Presbyterian Church of Watervliet," and March 29, it was organized as such by the Rev. Wm. H. Carr, who served for some time as pastor; the elders were Van Buren Lockrow and Daniel P. Sigourney. There was no regular pastor after Mr. Carr's services ended, and the pulpit was supplied by transient preachers until, in 1878, Rev. Robert Ennis was appointed stated supply and continued his services for about three years, or until 1880; after this no regular preaching until January, 1885, when Rev. Josiah Markle assumed charge and is now pastor. The society report 30 families, 23 members, with a sabbath school of 35 pupils. The church edifice is a frame building, and will seat 200. Present trustees J. T. Worth, Lewis Knapp, John Frost.

A union Sabbath-school is maintained at Loudonville, and a mission school at Menand's.

The cemeteries and grave yards, or old burial grounds, are numerous through the township. In the early settlement a custom prevailed in which each land holder reserved or appropriated a portion of his farm for family burial purposes, and the free interment of those who were destitute of enough of earth for their last resting place. Often the church lot was a grave yard. At the present time many of these once hallowed grounds have fallen into disuse, and neglect marks the spot where molder the dust of forgotten ancestry.

With the progress that marks this age of human plans, there is a higher estimate given to this matter of the final resting place for the dead, and now a better and more enduring system is adopted, by corporations or associations organized in accordance with statute laws, for the purchase and perpetual maintainance of cemeteries, these to be sacredly used and carefully guarded, forever, for the burial of the human race.

The most important incorporated cemetery grounds located in this town are: the Albany Rural Cemetery, the St. Agnes, and the Anshe Emeth, which are north of Albany City about three miles, on the line of the Watervleit Turnpike and Horse Railway, and Delaware and Hudson Canal Companies Railroad. For a full notice of these cemeteries, see history of Albany City. The Evangelican Lutheran Church has a cemetery on the Sand Creek road (this is now within the city line), and St. Patrick's Catholic Church has one on the Albany and Schenctady Turnpike.

The Shakers have a cemetery, in which none but members of their society are interred. In this plain and unadorned inclosure, Mother Ann Lee was buried.

THE HOME FOR AGED MEN—The ladies who conceived this charity, and who were instrumental in pressing its claims upon the attention of the public, were: Mrs. Elizabeth McClure, Mrs. William B. Gourlay and Mrs. Cornelius Ten Broeck; and through the persistent personal efforts of William Sawyer and other friends, who became interested in the benevolent project, the founding of this institution was accomplished. This is one of the fruits of Christianity; for no home for the aged, for orphans, no hospital for the poor was ever seen in any but in a Christian nation. After sufficient interest was manifested, a public meeting was held in its behalf in November, 1874, in the Second Presbyterian Church, and an eloquent sermon, appropriate to the occasion, was preached by Rev. Ebenezer Halley, D. D., to a large and interested audience. At the conclusion of the exercises it was announced that at a previous meeting an organization had been effected and officers elected.

Subscriptions continued to be solicited and made in aid of the charity, which gave assurance that success would finally crown these patient exertions.

During the autumn of 1876, subscriptions amounted to about $18,000, and on the fifth day of October, 1876, the articles of incorporation were effected, and the society duly and legally organized, with name and object as follows: "We, the undersigned residents of the County of Albany, do hereby associate ourselves together for the purpose of forming a benevolent and charitable society, the name of which society shall be, 'The Home for Aged Men,' and its particular object shall be the relief, care, culture and support of needy or dis-

942   HISTORY OF THE COUNTY OF ALBANY.

tressed old men and their wives, of the said County of Albany."

The following gentlemen were named trustees in the certificate of incorporation: Messrs. John Taylor Cooper, Maurice E. Viele, William Sawyer, S. Visscher Talcott, Dudley Olcott, Ebenezer Halley, William M. Van Antwerp, Benjamin W. Arnold, James H. McClure, James B. Jermain, Jeremiah Waterman and David A. Thompson.

Upon the organization of the board of trustees, John Taylor Cooper was elected President, James B. Jermain and Jeremiah Waterman, Vice-Presidents, Dudley Olcott, Treasurer, and David A. Thompson, Secretary.

On the 16th of November, 1876, the trustees purchased the residence and grounds of Mrs. Harriet Day Perry, situated between the Watervliet turnpike and railway on the east, and the Rensselaer and Saratoga Railroad on the west, a short distance south 'of Menand's road. The distance from the north city line is less than two miles, and is reached by the horse or steam cars.

The price paid for the dwelling and about four acres of land was $11,000, and the total cost of the alterations, additions and necessary improvements amount to $20,000.

The location is high and commanding, with an extensive view up and down the Hudson River, and over a large tract of beautifully diversified country. The original buildings were of antique structure, with high rooms and high ceilings, which gave evidence of comfort and repose. The old mansion—built in 1781—has been remodeled to correspond to modern architecture and meet the design of its purposes in all its appointments. The grounds were graded and tastefully arranged; a clean, attractive lawn surrounds the buildings.

The "Home" was dedicated March 28, 1878, and has accommodations for thirty persons. "The object of the Home is to provide for respectable men, who at an advanced age are left helpless and alone in the world, and whose poverty is due to misfortune rather than to idleness or vice."

Every applicant must furnish satisfactory testimonials of good character, and must implicitly obey all the rules and regulations of the society or trustees.

The associate officers of the patronesses of the Home are: Mrs. Howard Townsend, President; Mrs. William Barnes, Vice-President ; Miss Mary G. Rice, Treasurer ; Miss Susan Dunlap, Matron in charge.

EDUCATION.—SCHOOLS.

In the early settlement of this township, difficulties, almost insurmountable, operated for many years to retard every effort for the advancement of popular education. The facilities were only within reach of the few, and these were not eager to avail themselves of the private means that were required for other and more immediate purposes. The want of means and opportunity were the great obstacles these people had to contend with in their mental and spiritual training ; being distant from the centers of social and intellectual culture, they were dependent upon local and simple expedients for first principles in elementary education. These were improved as best they could, and in time their means were concentrated and pupils were collected in private schools ; these were imperfectly organized, and not until after the revolution did the schools assume much importance, when State authority gave them aid and encouragement, and they were incorporated in a system that has really educated the children of the State. The effect of this change is to insure to all the advantages of a common education, and a free discussion of questions that concern a higher education ; and at the present time, a knowledge of the elements of general science and the laws of mechanics and industrial art, and the philosophy of natural sciences in their relation to the laws under which we live, and which concern the immediate welfare and usefulness of every individual.

The great design of popular education should be to develop and train the faculties for the useful pursuits of life, in connection with mental culture, for the scientific investigation and study of sciences and philosophy, practical mechanics, and manual industries for the development of human skill. Are sudden and novel changes of method or system always attended with success? Do the improved educational systems give better results for the full comprehension of important discoveries that will enable the pupil to appreciate theories as truths that contain real wisdom ? Systems of moral and mental progress, theories of religious revelations and political traditions are problems yet to pass the ordeal of modern science and revealed truth.

At the time Watervliet was formed as a township, the schools had no system or organization, and were conducted by private or individual enterprise. It is evident that results from this imperfect method could not be of a high order, as only the more favored children could enjoy the benefits derived from the limited means offered.

There seems to have been very little interest manifested in the education of the children in the rural districts, until 1795, when the State gave Albany County £1,590, equal to $3,975, for school purposes, of which the townships then organized received their proportion. This was the first step toward our free school system, which has developed to such magnificent results, and grand practical returns have followed the wise legislation of the State in securing popular education to the masses.

In September, 1813, Watervliet divided the township into 12 school districts, giving each a certain number of families, and the only geographic boundary was the division line of the farms owned by occupants mentioned, and this condition exists with many of the districts at the present time.

It is well to note the marked difference in the schools of the rural districts, and contrast their inefficiency with those of the city. Graded systems and methods can only be taught successfully and with the best results by teachers who introduce a system, and by personal supervision through a continuous term of several years, thus introducing an arrangement or specific plan of instruction, that can be followed from grade to grade and class to class, without breaking the order or introducing *new* or widely different methods.

If the schools in the rural districts have a lower standard of efficiency or usefulness than the city district schools, the fault can be attributed in a great measure to the mistakes of trustees, who from economy, custom or some petty cause change teachers at every term, thereby retarding progress in studies and losing time in reorganizing. This constant change demoralizes the school for many weeks of the term, and in the end the teacher is pronounced a failure, and the pupils have made very little progress, for nothing is learned of value by continuous changes.

Watervliet at present is divided into 27 districts, and during the school year which closed August 20, 1884, fifty-nine teachers were employed in these schools.

A table is given of the condition of these schools for the above school year, which shows a marked contrast for the past and present.

The number of school districts September 30, 1869, was 28, employing 59 teachers. Number of children of school age, 14,076; number attending school, 7,400; amount expended for school purposes, $67,292.03. This, perhaps, includes schools of Cohoes.

No. of District.	Persons of School Age.	Number Attended School.	Valuation of District.	Amount of Receipts.	Amount Paid Teachers.	Paid Teacher for Winter Term.	Paid Teacher for Summer Term.
1	1,115	496	$1,155,400	$5,118 69	$3,085 31	$14 00	$14 00
2	1,032	556	697,666	4,596 29	2,585 00	......	......
3	22	16	162,361	486 77	340 80	10 00	9 00
4	27	14	......	......	......	......	......
5	58	35	198,249	439 54	296 20	8 00	8 00
6	68	42	223,502	386 56	286 80	10 00	8 00
7	48	22	160,672	290 17	241 60	9 00	8 00
8	54	16	204,700	266 53	237 00	12 00	12 00
9	1,317	210	430,000	1,555 65	1,100 00	10 00	8 50
10	77	40	228,742	345 40	286 50	6 00	4 00
11	185	88	374,296	1,186 06	840 00	10 00	7 00
12	81	48	129,250	297 00	240 66	8 00	7 00
13	61	36	128,850	430 93	264 00	......	......
14	34	28	215,000	259 89	206 25	......	......
15	200	95	384,358	1,467 34	897 90	......	......
16	39	34	247,574	300 09	240 00	......	......
17	109	72	108,497	377 87	306 00	8 50	8 50
18	54	45	185,500	433 50	278 50	7 00	9 00
19	230	154	996,897	2,180 66	1,215 00	33 75	33 75
20	843	500	1,047,015	4,085 07	2,250 05	......	......
21	80	62	76,860	546 43	321 00	10 00	7 00
22	277	62	1,726,514	754 80	485 90	12 50	12 50
23	1,283	898	1,738,640	10,562 94	6,560 10	12 50	15 50
24	76	53	107,603	450 77	255 00	......	......
25	84	44	112,740	466 66	288 00	9 00	6 00
26	83	64	197,853	460 11	335 00	8 00	6 00
27	40	23	113,117	1,004 03	309 76	......	......
Totals,	7,651	3,755	$9,848,757	$38,726 75	$23,743 23		

SOLDIERS.

During the Revolutionary war, soldiers and munitions were transported along the London road from Albany to Saratoga. No battles were fought on the soil of the *Vlakte,* yet Morgan's men encamped for the winter in the northeast part of the town, and his men quartered on the farmers in the vicinity of the Boght. Here the Indians and Tories held council and plotted mischief against their neighbors, and gave aid to the British. The deeds and service rendered by Gen. Schuyler, and the active part which he so patriotically performed in the struggle of the colony for liberty, will be found in the County history and in the history of West Troy.

Henry Ostrom, who settled on the Capron farm, was a captain of militia. Served under Gen. Van Rensselaer in the Mohawk valley, about the time of Burgoyne's surrender. Jacob and Gerret Lansing were soldiers in this war that gave us independence from the rule of Great Britain.

In the war of 1812, Watervliet furnished a large quota of volunteers and drafted men, among whom were Henry Runkle, Frederick Roff,* John G. Lansing, John Van Aernum, Lansing Fonda, John Cory, David Turner, Jacob Lewis, William Campbell, Jacob Turner, John Steenbergh and brother, Timothy Hodgeman, Stephen Culver, Jeremiah and Gerret Clute, Wynant Van Denbergh. The following entry is copied from records in the Town Clerk's office: "Andrew Chadwick enlisted as a soldier, September, 1812, and died on the 13th of

---

*Since the above was written, Peter Shaver, of Guilderland, has died, aged 90 years. He was drafted at the same time with Frederick Roff, and assigned to the same company.

HISTORY OF THE COUNTY OF ALBANY.

December, 1812, in the service at Champlain. Benjamin Burdsall, Captain United States Volunteers." Frederick Roff, now 90 years old, in good health and memory, yet deprived of eyesight and partially deaf, was drafted and sent to Long Island in 1814. Peace was declared soon after, and he returned to his home after three months' absence. He served under Captain Van Wie, of Bethlehem. Mr. Roff receives a pension, and is the only living soldier of the war of 1812 the author met in the five townships visited by him.

In the war of the Rebellion, Watervliet furnished her quota of officers and volunteers, and the record bears a favorable comparison with that of other townships of the county. The first act of hostility roused the loyalty and patriotism of the people to prompt action, and the zeal and devotion for the preservation of their country as a free and united nation awoke within their hearts the spirit of self-denial, and the loyal youth and mature manhood were ready to enlist; to exchange the comforts of home for the tented field and ensanguined battle ground; to give their lives, if needs be, for the safety of that freedom bought aforetime with the blood and treasure of their ancestors.

The patriotism so nobly manifested at the outbreak of this war was at no time allowed to cool, although many reverses and sad experiences fell to the lot of some. Those who lived to return from this horrible war proved themselves worthy of the cause—deserve lasting gratitude and generous remembrance for all time for their faithful services and sacrifices.

It were well if these officers and soldiers had a carefully prepared record in the archives of the township for future reference and inspection by those who, in after years, could learn the names and deeds, fate and sufferings of those who will soon be forgotten. There seems to have been a degree of indifference in this matter by the authorities, as the Legislature of 1865 enacted a law for this very purpose. At the present time such a record would be difficult to compile or obtain, yet the work should be attempted in some satisfactory way.*

CORPORATIONS, ASSOCIATIONS, RAILROADS, TURNPIKES, ETC.

Surprising changes followed the declaration which secured independence to a people who had long been under the rule of colonial taxation, and burdens that operated with severity against freedom of enterprise; these removed, men were ready to extend the bounds of settlement, and open new fields of enterprise, manufactures and trade. Men of means saw the necessity of greater facility of transportation of goods and crops, and set to work to obtain them.

To obtain this, in 1792 the "Northern Inland Lock and Navigation Company" was chartered, by which goods and merchandise were forwarded from the central part of the State and Lake Ontario by way of the Mohawk River to Schenectady, and thence to Albany by wagon. From here merchandise was sent to New York by river craft. A road to communicate with Cherry Valley, Utica and Rome had been in use for many years, and in 1798 an act was passed to establish a "Turnpike Corporation" for improving the State road. This act was afterward repealed, and March 15, 1799, an act was passed to establish a "Turnpike Corporation" for improving the State road from the house of John Weaver in Watervliet to Cherry Valley. The capital was two hundred shares at ten dollars each. This was the western turnpike. The incorporators were William North, John Taylor, Abram Ten Eyck, Charles R. Webster, Calvin Cheeseman, Zenas Penio, Ephraim Hudson, Joseph White, Elihu Phinney, Thomas Machin.

December 21, 1801, a bill was prepared and presented to the Legislature with this preface: Whereas, Goldbrow Bangor, Abraham Ten Broeck, Abraham Ten Eyck and others have entered into an association to form a company for making a turnpike road between the cities of Albany and Schenectady, March 30, 1802, etc. A bill was passed constituting John Lansing, Jr., Stephen Van Rensselaer, Stephen Lush, Dudley Walsh, Garret W. Van Schaick, Daniel Hall, John Tayler, Abraham Oadthout and Joseph C. Yeates, a body corporate and politic, by the name of "The President, Directors and Company of Albany and Schenectady Turnpike." The above incorporators were the first directors, with John Lansing, Jr., President; Barent Bleecker, Secretary and Treasurer; Garret Clute, Surveyor; the capital stock was $200,000; length of road, sixteen miles, commencing on Lodge street, up State to Washington street, and thence to Schenectady, in a straight line; the width of the road, four rods; roadbed, two rods wide, filled with stone, covered with sand or gravel; the ditches to be made wide enough for sleighs. This new road was not to interfere with the old State road between these two cities. During the construction of this road, $118,610 was expended, or about $8,472 per mile, and at its completion was considered the best road in the country.

The increased travel with heavy loads soon made an impression into the yielding material, and the company then made a roadbed of cobble stone brought from the Mohawk River, which was covered with gravel and held from spreading by stone curbing, and a thick flag stone was put on the roadbed for the wheels to run upon. This has proved of great utility, and the improvement cost the company $61,810, or about $4,415 per mile.

In 1803 the company commenced planting ten thousand Lombardy poplars along the sides of this road; only a few remain.

The construction of this road, as an internal or public improvement, was at the time one of great magnitude, and for many years was a financial success to the company; but upon the completion of the Erie Canal, that water-way at once secured the bulk of merchandise and produce for transportation, and the wagon road lost its source of its

---

* The original returns of the census of 1865, preserved in the New York State Library, contain (nominally, at least) lists of soldiers furnished by each town in the State for this war.

practice, many are enjoying their lives while wearing the name of Jesus, but refusing to wear His nature.

The church is being bombarded with same-sex couples and openly gay members and church leaders, users of recreational drugs, alcoholics and any other blatant sins known to humanity. The obvious overlooking or acceptance of such behaviors are the direct result of fear and selfishness. The ones that dare to preach the truth in love concerning these types of practices are quickly stereotyped as being intolerant, homophobic or modern-day judges. Since most of us do not want to be considered within this minority, we look the other way, as if it does not exist.

The only problem with that is, if we are not given the truth, we are rendered helpless in the spiritual warfare, which engages everyone (Eph 6:1-12, KJV).[3] John 8:32 says "and ye shall know the truth, and the truth shall make you free." Therefore, the only way that one will be free from the snare of the wicked is that they hear and respond to the truth. The truth is in the Word of God, and it is by our interest in, internalizing of, and intentionality in practicing the truth that our faith in God is fortitude (Rom 10:17, KJV).

Because a significant number of churchgoers appear not to be interested in the truth enough to internalize God's word, their intent is towards pleasing themselves and not God. In 2 Corinthians 4:3-4 Paul makes a very good observation, he says "but if our gospel be hid, it is hid to them that are lost: In whom the god of this world hath blinded the minds of them which believe not, lest the light of the glorious gospel of Christ, who is the image of God, should shine unto them." This type of behavior is known as willful blindness.

Because of spiritual blindness, many have been profoundly engaged and pulled into the, me, myself, and, I ministry, which entails the use of God's name to get all that they want out of this life. It seems that a vast majority that are named as being Christian are not trying to glorify God or expand His kingdom, nor are they hungering after souls in need of salvation. However, they are more

---

[3] Unless otherwise noted, all biblical passages referenced are in the *King James version* (Chattanooga, TN: AMG Publishers, 1996).

interested in building platforms for personal growth and gain, while ignoring the fact that an inevitable and abrupt end is nearing. It appears that many are preoccupied with avoiding the concept and conversation of Eschatology.

Millard J. Erickson in his book, *Christian Theology*, speaks briefly about the study of eschatology. Eschatology is the study of last things. Erickson presents the following four popular views of eschatology, based on the historical writings found in the books of Daniel, Matthew, and Revelation:[4]

> 1. Futuristic View ~ The events claimed are coming in the future.
>
> 2. Preterist View ~ The events took place at the time of the writing and are past.
>
> 3. Historical View ~ The events were to occur in the future at the time of the writing but are to unfold during the history of the church, and possibly are still unfolding now.
>
> 4. Symbolic View ~ The events are not to be considered in a time sequence at all.

There is not enough time within this writing to discuss each view in detail. What is most important is that whatever stance a person takes, that they not be found on the adverse side of the conversation as spoken by Jesus in Matthew 7:21-23 concerning the judgement. As I read this text, Jesus is not talking to non-believers. It appears that Jesus is speaking with individuals holding positions in the church, even as leaders because we do not usually see the average layperson prophesying, or casting out devils, or other miraculous works. Some have somehow made their way into a prominent

---

[4] Millard J. Erickson, *Christian Theology*, (Grand Rapid, MI: Baker Academic, 2013), 1060.

role in the Christian community, just to get to Judgement to hear Jesus say, "I never knew you."[5] Unfortunately, these sad words are not only reserved for those in prominent positions, but it is to all that refuse to surrender to the Word, Will, and Way of God.

I understand that in this technological age in which we live, sin seems to be more prevalent and available to us, but so is the Holy Spirit. God told us in Deuteronomy 31:8 and in Hebrews 13:5 that "He would never leave nor forsake us." Then He showed us in Hebrews 13:8 that "Jesus is the same yesterday, today and forever." Although it seems as if times have changed and that in general, our current state of morality has hit an all-time low, those of us who know the truth must stand firm on the Word of God. 1 Corinthians 10:13 states, "There hath no temptation taken you but such as is common to man: but God is faithful, who will not suffer you to be tempted above that ye are able; but will with the temptation also make a way to escape, that ye may be able to bear it." Which simply means, we will be tempted, tried, and tested, but not beyond measure. Jesus said in John 16:33 "These things I have spoken unto you, that in me ye might have peace. In the world ye shall have tribulation: but be of good cheer; I have overcome the world." Which agrees with the previous text of scripture, whatever comes our way, as long as we stand in God we shall overcome. Colossians 3:3 says "For ye are dead, and your life is hid with Christ in God."

According to the Scriptures, an end to the world as we know it is soon approaching. So, it behooves everyone on the face of the earth to align themselves with the Word of God. It has been said on many occasions, there is a Heaven and a Hell, and you cannot miss them both.

---

[5] Matthew 7:23.

CHAPTER SEVEN

Charlie Redden

About Me: Charlie Redden

Favorite Scripture:
Proverbs 27:1-2
Boast not thyself of to morrow; for thou knowest not what a day may bring forth. 2. Let another man praise thee; and not thine own mouth; a stranger, and not thine own lips.

Pet Peeves:
"Pretenders!" Someone that betray themselves of not who they truly are. Impatient with slow and inattentive drivers.

Favorite Foods:
Caribbean Cuisine, Grilled Chicken, and Seafood.

Skills/Talents:
Professional Chef
Play the Piano, trumpet and some brass instruments
Short Story & Poetry Writer
Food & Ice Sculpturer

Hobbies:
Listening to Gospel Soloists & Classical Music
Raising Aquarium Fish
Watching past Dallas Cowboys Games
Spending time at the Shore

Favorite Vacation Place:
Botswana, Africa
various places within the Caribbean

New Home Baptist Church Poetic Voices Ministry

Awakened to the Questions Not Yet Answered

    Question! Can anyone assemble here today, please tell me, what kind of reward is it profitable for a man or a woman to gain when he or she is not yet Kingdom ready? Or even still, how does a song with the sweetest melody heal a heart that has been broken to pieces time after time again and again? But most importantly, to you my Lord, where have all the precious flowers gone? Did you wither them to sleep away beneath the crust of the earth to again one day rise, and blossom to sleep no more? Now awaken thy spirit of hope! I mean why must you hide yourself behind the shadows of shame when a lonely and unwanted child cries out loud inside beyond the midnight hour, frightened and frigid from mental and physical pain. Even more over than that, can someone among us today please tell me, where does the mockingbird sings when there is no harmony of peace? Oh, awaken I say ye sisters, thy virtuous woman, I mean why give up the best of your temple to a brother that has never promised you a divine sense of comfort or stability. Oh, waken I say, thy spirit of mankind! For how can flowing waters and flames of desire ignite that faith within, when the spirit and legacy of our father and his father's father, has been forgotten?

    Forgotten that fertile ground and its foundation should not be made by hands alone but by the blood, sweat, and tears from a generation that purges itself in the business of dignity and united strength that binds the faith and the multitude of people together as one. So hear this beloved, there is going to rise a time of a day when the lilies of the valley will gain it's strength to stand against the gust of the strongest winds. They will awaken with all of the precious of flowers that went before us. Oh who among us will be there? Will it be that old gospel preacher that saved generations of lives, but in the end couldn't do anything to help or save himself? Yes, who among us will be there to flourish in the faith and legacy of our father father's, and his father father's. Oh that blest day, when each and every one of us will be able to say, I saw the mocking bird sing. I comforted the lonely child after the midnight hour; saw the precious flowers blossom at sunrise; sat and had supper with that old gospel preacher who thought he was doomed to the gates of hell. But, watch this now. Which one us will find ourselves stranded and left behind in the scorching fires of eternal death? Which one among us will that be? So, my prayer and earnest plea to you my Lord, is that each and every one of us can awaken one day, not focusing so deep towards the questions not yet answered, but to the very purpose and the will that drives this wicked world to nonexistence. Which one of us will that be? Oh, awaken I say! Awaken!

Better Days Ahead

My Lord, I'm so proud and honored to have you in my life, for
You will always be.
Nothing can compare to the sweet drops of strength. You pour
deep inside of my soul.
I get strong every time I think of the wonderful blessing that
You've bestowed.
With these blessings my Beloved, there's nothing but, better
days ahead.
There was a time in my life, when peace like a river was not the
order of the day.
I would lean to my own understanding;[107] thinking I had everything all under control. Me for me. I for myself.
You see the common things and the things to the heart, it didn't
matter at all. But when the Spirit of the Living God
invaded the principles of my true integrity.
It was only then, that I can run, and not be worried; sing and
never get tired, and shout my troubles over. Always leaving room
for the Spirit of humility.
Oh, I say, and I say again, to all of my beloved ones to me. inside
each and every one of us,
there is a Spirit of a mighty warrior with the ability to sore
like an eagle, conquering any mountain, way beyond our
wildest dreams.
A group of saints and soldiers that can come together as one
body in Christ, build on nothing else
then Jesus blood and righteousness.[108]
And in the midst of this great sanctuary of peace; Yes, Oh
Yes, there is a fountain that is filled with blood, drawn from
Emmanuel's veins and sinners plunged
beneath that flood and lose all their guilty stains.[109]

Oh, who among us can ever deny the faith and the measure of
the Father's Love; when the children of Israel
was to be led out of the land of Egypt under
the harsh ruling of Pharaoh, into a new land of promise. Was
not it the same God that brought them through? And when the
children of the villages of Kakamega, Nambali, and Bungoma of
West Kenya, Africa
needed shoes upon their feet; it was not the same God
that provided?
And through the sweat, tears, and sometimes fear of over 50 years
of existence in this great place;
was it not the same God that brought us through and provided?
My beloved one to me, yes there are better days ahead.
But in order to reach that destiny of desire, we must constantly
"strive for the advancement of this church;
To religiously educate our children, and our children's children;
To avoid all tattling, back biting, and excessive anger.
To be slow to take offense, but always ready for reconciliation; To
be mindful of the rules of our Savior Jesus."[110]
Jesus who is The Christ of every man, woman, boy, and girl.
Keeping in mind that, He is Alpha and Omega, the beginning
and The End, The First and The Last, Jehovah Jira, our only
Provider, Prince of Peace, Lord of Lords, and King of Kings.[111]
Breathe on us now, my beloved Lord;
The breath of Life that we might soar like eagles[112]
at mornings dew; until the sun goes down. We'll worship You.
Tis morning come again, as we rise from our bed.
It is what it is. Better days ahead.

Dwelling Together In Divine Unity

My Lord, what a morning? And again, the sunshine has greeted me with the warmth of its loving kindness. And unto you my blessed redeemer, I pledge my legion to you for the things that you have already done, to the things that has not yet been birthed. Oh! How sweet it is when I think of the waters of Africa, how the warm mellow winds gently massages the surface of the sea; transforming the elements of nature to dance together as one. Now one can only imagine that even in the darkest despair of mankind, that there is a sense of divine holiness that has a spirit within itself to unite a culture or maybe a generation of people. Then and now, to a dwelling place of perfect peace. A divine level of peace, where those who gather at the waters will one day look deep down inside of their souls and wonder how I made it over. Even when the tides that binds us together as one in His name; so is He with us even forever more. So, cover us this day oh Lord, cover us with your tender mercies and loving kindness.113 For it is only you alone that we abide our trust upon, for what man on this earth can do the things that you do? Calm the raging sea, give hope to the hopeless, turn night into day and day into night, form the earth into a display of wonder, season to season, make a way out no way, speak to the winds telling them to behave, and to us with a great thunder letting us know that the wages of sin is still death, but the gift of God is eternal life.114 Oh hear me beloved as I say this day. It is time for us in these last and evil days on earth to gather at the waters and lay aside all the hurtful differences that retards the inner soul from spiritual nourishment. For the time that knows us now will soon know no more. For one day the mortal soul will be flushed away into the crust of its earth, vanishing like a puff of smoke into the winds of time. For unto us, behold He who keeps Israel shall neither slumber nor sleep, for the Lord is your keeper, Oh! Safe in His arms where the sun shall not strike you by day, nor the moon by night for He shall preserve thy soul, your going out and your coming in from this day forth, and even forever more.115 So I say to us in this great sanctuary this day, all the way to the great sanctuary in France, Bien-aime, pour moi demeure dansl' unite divine de le seigneur est le moyen da la render droite, simply meaning, Oh my beloved to me, dwelling together in divine unity is the Lord's way of making it right. For there's no better sense of perfect peace, in mind body and soul then dwelling together in divine unity.

New Home Baptist Church Poetic Voices Ministry

THE WEDDING
"For Better or Worse, I Still Choose You"

Baby, I remember the very first time that I laid eyes upon you. It was there and only then that my whole world which was once shattered began to pick up the pieces of my broken emptiness. You see, now I could've easily given up my faith and my desires for another, but for better or worse with you, I am totally COMPLETE. So, this day, this moment, and even at this very hour, I hum and sing a new melody now; a melody so sweet that the angels on high can't even comprehend. Oh my precious one to me, I find a heart within you even more precious than gold that out measures more than anything that I can ever imagine. Even the very scent of you, reminds me of the freshest and sweetest perfumes imported from Africa. There's something about your love that drives me wild and makes me weak; even when I'm at my strongest point. So come with me beloved; let us walk hand in hand and rest below a rare willow tree, along the shore, until the evening sun descend beneath the crests of its earth, all the way to the morning sun peeks beyond the horizon at the early break of dawn. And let not the troubles of your heart over take the sensitivity of your inner strength, because if it does; I'll be that bridge over troubled water is to catch you when you fall; that rock that shall not be moved, for I am with you even until the end of time. So, as our yolks equally bind and seal itself together as one, you know… you for me and me for you. Let us take His yolk upon us and learn of Him for His yolk is easy and His burdens are light.[116] So, this day, this moment, and even at this very hour, my shattered dreams, my desires for another, your walk, your talk, the very scent of you, me being that bridge over troubled water, my new melody, your golden heart. So to death do us part, I promise you this, even when I'm about to take my last breath upon the earth on my dying bed, "I'LL STILL BE LOVING YOU IN

MY ARMS." And it doesn't matter what they say, because say they will, but when it's all said and done, for better or worse… baby I still choose you.

FROM PAIN TO GAIN

Life can be so deceiving at times, sort of like an impulsive illusion you know. Especially, when the road ahead becomes too much to bear, so much, that it sometimes causes us to react to desperate measures. You know, that itch deep down inside that needs a scratch or just to lay and cuddle with someone through the night; or a little substance, anything or anybody just to take the pain away, that just won't leave us alone. Listen to this... have you ever thought what it would be like for the very first time, that's some of us of course, to go out, play the lottery and hit for 7 million dollars after taxes? Sounds like completion don't it? Or to finally go out, meet and marry that very person we always dreamed about. Oh, you know them! Just the right height, a little bit of thick here, a little bit thin there, tall dark and handsome, muscles and curves in all the right places. Someone that would probably make you lose your God given religion, but it doesn't matter.

Somebody! Anybody! that will take that pain and itch away that just won't leave us alone. But hear me beloved as I say this day; it seems in these times of desperate measures when the chips are down, the very thing that takes us back to square one is another human being that doesn't benefit the spirit of the heart to a higher level of faith. Oh! But the heart, it becomes no match in desperate measures when it is left unguarded. All of us heard of the fictional story of the "Big Bad Wolf and The Three Little Pigs." Well let me put a little twist to the story. You see the first little pig decided to guard her heart out of straw, with no hesitation, Mr. Smooth Bad Wolf, came along and blew the straw away from the pigs' heart. So, the second little pig saw what happened and decided to guard her heart out of sticks, low and behold, here he comes again, Mr. Smooth Bad Wolf. After several attempts, he successfully blew the sticks away from the second pig's heart. So just to say that there's nothing wrong with falling in love and opening your heart to the things that matters the most. But oh the mind; for the mind is such a terrible thing to waste;[117] which bring me to the third little pig who is very aware of what happen to her sisters and decided to guard her heart out of bricks. No sooner after that, here he comes again, Mr. Smooth Bad Wolf, with no hesitation he huffed and puffed with several attempts with all his might, but couldn't blow the bricks away from the third little pigs' heart. So, go ahead beloved, live life to the fullest, protect and build your hopes on things eternal and hold to God's unchanging hands.[118] For without pain, there is no gain.

New Home Baptist Church Poetic Voices Ministry

HEAVENLY BOUND

    Here I am oh Lord, and it seems my time on earth is almost at its end. Heavy is the weight that anchors me down, for in spite of all for my worried years, I am now at peace within; for yes, I am heavenly bound. So detain me and my heart oh Lord, and take me to that nesting place, a place where the sweet melody of the angels silhouette, rocks me to sleep in the arms of your precious touch. For no longer will my broken dreams be scattered amongst the earth, for they too will be laid to sleep beneath the pillow of my resting head. So tender is the night. So come with me oh Lord and let us walk hand in hand along the shore, to meet the horizon at its break. For it is then and only then that my fragile soul will be lifted up to heaven's gate. But before that descent oh Lord, there is something that I must say for the sake of mankind. And to this wicked world as I begin to depart , the signs of the time and the cry of the child's heart has solidified itself that Christ is soon to come. And if the inner spirit is not in order, aligning itself with the blood of Christ; it is certain that the last breath we take on earth will be doomed until the pits of a darken stream of agony and defeat. For what good is it that a man can gain the whole world just to lose his soul to selfish foolishness.[119] But here is the good news. Hear me beloved as I say and I say, when the great bells in Zion shall tone and we take unto the air our last quiet breath on the earth; let not your heart be trouble[120] for he that is in Him shall not perish and have ever lasting life.[121] So come ye that love the Lord and let the joy of the gospel be spread through the lands both near and far; proclaiming that Christ our savior is alive and well sitting on the right hand side of the Father.[122] He's still mending broken hearts, feeding the hungry, clothing the naked,[123] and protecting the very essence of the masters plea. So dare not trust the sweetest frame, but holy lean on His everlasting name.[124] Now with a made-up mind beloved, go hard after kingdom principles and never mind what they say for the Lord sits high and looks low; knowing your every move towards the freedom you've come to possess inside of you. So, fret not thy calling and purpose upon the earth, for there are better days ahead of you now. So be what it may, because I leave you with an array of hope. Oh, stand firm beloved with both feet planted on solid ground, for anything else is sinking sand; and with that foundation of a courageous spirit, you too, indeed are heavenly bound.

New Home Baptist Church Poetic Voices Ministry

Home Sweet Home

To my beloved family, I may be absent from the body,[125] but I'm so glad that you forgot me not. So many wonderful and fond memories will keep me rested at peace knowing that someday soon we will all meet up here and be crowned on that glorious day of victory. Through all of the wonderful and fond memories, how can any one of us ever forget the love and strength of family; the important thing that matters the most? When one got sick or failed at a certain endeavor, each and every one of us felt the pain deep down inside. But oh, the strength of family, how it kept us united as one through the good times as well as the bad from season to season. Summer morns, the smell of Sunday mornings dew would enhance the aroma of fresh brewed ground coffee and sweet homemade buttermilk blueberry biscuits which helped us prep ourselves as we got ready for Sunday morning service. And who can ever forget the memories of Autumn. The smell of cinnamon baked pumpkin and apple pie hot out of the oven as the crisp mellow winds would gently sway the colorful harvest and trees to dance together as one. And for winter's plea, how the holidays would put us in the spirit of youth that brought out the best in each and every one of us as the white and sparkling snow would cover its earth from land to land. The sight, the sound, the touch, the smell and the taste of winters offering would somehow keep all of us mindful that Christ was and still is the serenity of it all. And as the mellow spring invite itself upon the sea and sand of its shore; we would all anticipate new beginnings, like the fresh and crystal-clear waters from the springs and brooks that would cleanse its earth with a pure and unforgettable sense of hope. So yes, a time of reflection in healing is in order that we never forget the memories that brought us thus far. And with faith, God will keep us through; be it good times as well as the bad. And with that little bit of hope and precious peace, we hold deep inside; oh fear not beloved, because you are never alone; for there is no better place of healing than "home sweet home."

I Come To See

For there is no greater love then it is for a man or woman to lay down his or her very life for a friend.[126] So, this day come, this hour come, and at this moment, I come to see, to see if each and every one of you still had that spirit and legacy deep down inside that you forgot me not. You know it seems like only yesterday when the vivid memories will invade my spirit even as I rest in the arms of my Lord and Savior. So I say to you beloved, out of all of your hopes and dreams, never give up on who you truly are deep down inside your soul. Reach out to those who hunger for spiritual nourishment. Pay attention to that perfect peace within, and shadow not the things that disrupt your spirit of dignity. And hear me beloved, always tread the waters that bring you safely to shore. And never mind what they say! For no one knows the trouble you see. So, I come to see that those better days ahead of you now, will embrace and comfort you with the intimacy of care and affection. And remember no matter how hard and rough the road ahead of you get, I'll be with you always as long as you, forget me not. So, in the end, I rest in peace with great expectations knowing indeed that we will meet again. So, to each and every one of you, I will only hope and wish that better days will not only bring you perfect peace within, but a sense of direction simply knowing that you truly believe *a forgiving heart is the key to kingdom readiness*. Oh! Try it beloved! And just you wait and see. So, as I go now, I leave you with this, Oh! Fight a good fight! Finish the course! And keep the faith! For with these three elements, God almighty has a place like no other, "Heaven," for you to come and see.

LET HIS WILL BE DONE

Not long ago there was a certain kind of people that can endure some of the best of times as well as the worst of times. I mean, the capacity of what they could endure deep inside of their souls back then, would overwhelm some of us these days to a panic rage of fear. A fear that would ultimately cripple and test the very faith of some believers to think twice about if God is really real. Back then, they were destined; and it was inevitable that this kind of people, the people of "Homead Place," that they merged and purged themselves together as one with a mindset of enhancing while advancing to a whole new level of faith. Now in these days we've gotten to a place where science, technology and social media has become the new God to some believers and that with these three elements, why even wait upon a true and living God at that pace when just about everything is now at the touch of a button. For us, it is refreshing to know that the true and living God that we serve is still and will forever be Alpha and omega and the author and finisher of all things big and small.[127] Nevertheless, no matter how some believe or speculate, the winds will constantly blow, the seas will always rumble at the feet of its shore, a brown cow will always eat green grass and produce white milk, and the mountains will remain at its highest height until God says, "It's done." So, the question is asked to each and every one of us, "What does it truly mean to throw away childish things?" Or to love the Lord thy God with all thy heart, and with all thy soul, and with all thy mind?"[128] Well it simply means, "Freedom," and with that freedom, self-dignity begins to triumph and usher in "better things for better people", "enhancing while advancing"[129] to the things that matters the most. Yes for some, life is going to be what it truly is. A sweet mellow melody will always pierce the hearts of those who hunger for peace. A curious child will always thirst for wisdom and knowledge from a mother's love that nurtures a virtuous admiration towards better days ahead. Now if these things are to be true, how is it remotely possible for a group of soldiers, like us, in the same army to come together fighting for a common cause in defeating an adversary that is so strong; that even sometime a cry and relief from heaven on high is no more than a figment of one's imagination, "THE BIBLE?" From the book of Proverbs 29:18 states, "*where there is no vision the people perish,* but he that keepeth the law, happy is he." Well the law has been kept and the vision is guiding us straight ahead, but in order for us as one to enhance this law and vision in defeating the adversary, the mindset like in the days of old, would have to get in gear of understanding that there are sometimes two types of people in this world, "MOVERS AND SHAKERS." Now a mover is one who would stop at nothing in seeing things all the way through and that the progress is to reach its highest potential towards the will of mankind. Now the shaker is one that no matter what the opposition is, he or she bears the strength deep inside to absorb and shake off any weapons formed against them. But imagine this beloved, what if all of us had the ability and the capacity to inherit both, a mover and a shaker?

OH! The faith of such power will ignite the very heights from heaven above causing our Lord to sweep down and breathe upon us like never before; flowing through the hearts of doubt, cliques, selfishness, and envy. Now let's think about it. God has been so good to all of us through the best of times as well as the worst of times and no matter how hard we try, we just can't beat His giving. That day on Calvary, Jesus was willing to go all the way. For what greater love it takes for a man to lay down his very life for a friend.[130] Now for us, God knows the true person He created. For He knew us back then, from the time we were created; a seed to birth and He was elated. Now in His eyes, a creation like no other. He completed His task; no need to go further. Yes, even you beloved, a precious masterpiece, an angel to behold, never let it cease. So, what He has made, never take it for granted, for you are completely different throughout His planet. So, be strong brave heart, staying faithful and true for there is a balm in Gilead[131] deep inside of you. Now let Him order our steps[132] and let us not lean not to our own understanding,[133] constantly asking, "What God can do for us, but instead, asking Him what we can do for Him and the kingdom?" Jesus paid the ultimate sacrifice for the master's plea. Now the victory has been won. Now the question is, "how far are we willing to go just to let his will be done?"

Rumble in the Jungle

There comes a time in each and every one of our lives that a realization sticks and it hits home. A realization that break throughs ain't free. Even after a succession of fasting and praying, still the victory is not even beyond the horizon. A so-called victory that somehow knocks us right back to where we started from. I mean the agony of defeat, now becomes a pattern, a pattern of maybe just another 5th of Vodka, a bag of weed, a couple hits of Remy Martin VSOP, or even maybe a couple lines of cocaine. You know just a little stimulant to take the edge off a bit. My God! How long? And when does it end? The pain sometime is so deep that I wish that the Lord would place His head upon my chest of what's left of my beating heart. But, know one thing for sure, that no matter how young or old, there's a pregnancy inside each and every one of us that is about to birth into something spectacular. So why idle thy precious time away hoping for a miracle that has already happened. They say, "Not today! Maybe come back tomorrow." And how many times have we heard that again and again? But, know that it is written beloved, for as long as the dew drops of mercy, shine bright upon me by day and by night, I shall not be denied.[134] So, back off, I say thy spirit of laziness and you too I say thy spirit of procrastination, for it is time for me to rumble. So the announcer says, "In this corner, we have at 4 feet nothing, 80 pounds soaking wet, by way of New Home Baptist Church. His name is disappointed, abused, talked about, mistreated, lied on, spat upon, and no go for nothing, all time loser with no faith to be found." And his opponent, in the next corner, standing at 6 feet forever, weighing in at 250 pounds of solid muscles, by way of the hands of God. He never lost a battle. He stood up face to face, strong, unmovable, abounding in faith, courageous as David, cutting off the head of Goliath. And the opponent of the New Home fighter is….."Himself."

The Midnight Hour

Not to long after the midnight hour, I had a dream that an angel awoke me from my sleep and asked if I was ready? Surprised and with a bewildered look upon my face, the angel calmly and quickly said unto me, "oh no beloved! It's not your time as of yet. My visit was to come and ask you if the rapture was to take place in the next 24 hours, will you be ready?" So, with deep thought, it was revealed to me what the angel was saying. Even now and until the end of time, many shall run to and fro and the knowledge of man will increase tremendously, but there is going to come a time in a little while when the great bells of Zion shall tone; calling the hearts of man to finally surrender. Many sinners and nonbelievers at the last second will try and seek refuge in the arms of the Comforter, but it will be too late because the rapture would've already taken place. So, the warning is very clear to the hearts of mankind.

Matthew 24:33 states, *"so likewise ye, when ye shall see all things know that it is near, even at the doors like also it was in the days of Lot, they did eat, they drank, they brought, they sold, they planted, and they build."* 2 Timothy 2:3 states, *"For men shall be lovers of them own selves, covetous, boasters, proud, blasphemies, disobedient to parents, unthankful, unholy, even shall it be in the day when the son of man is revealed."* Still to this day no man knows the hour or the day, when Christ shall come.[135] So, the question is asked to each and every one of us, if the rapture was to take place in the next 24 hours, will we be ready? For this generation shall not pass until all is fulfilled. So, with the full armor of God, let us stand our post faithful and true; and be on guard for the midnight hour.

How Long? Not Long, The Secret Garden of Prayer

It's me again Lord, here at mornings dew just before the sun is about to rise and give it's dawning of a new day. And in spite of all my imperfections, my inner spirit constantly aches to be in the presence of your everlasting beauty. For there is a place, a place where the rumbling seas humbles itself beneath the hem of your garment. And me, I'll hasten myself to dwell with thee for there's no place else I'd rather be. That is, the secret garden of prayer.

There my Lord, I am finally free, free and surrounded by the ambience and the sweet aroma of Mother Nature's brew. When I am restless and tired, I am then cradled and rocked fast asleep like a newborn child, safe, sound and secure in the love of his father's arms. And when I am physically hungry, I am fed daily with the warm inviting taste of milk and sweet honey upon my lips for there's no place else I'd rather be, that is, the secret garden of prayer.

Before that place, my Lord, I would find myself scattered about the earth trying desperately hard to find myself scattered about the earth, trying desperately hard to find someone to love me for me, but each time that I would surrender my heart to the forbidden passions of my women's plea, I'd find myself right back where I started from. That is, the secret garden of prayer.

How long Lord should I have subjected myself to the agony of defeat hoping that the woman would one day come and twine with me as one? Well, today the spirit inside of me says, it's not long. But, in the midst of my waiting, there is a question that is not yet answered by the spirit of man. That is, how long? How long should the African child walk amongst the earth with no shoes upon his feet? Well! It's not long. And how long Lord, should an innocent young girl or an innocent young boy fall victim to the prohibited touch of hands that was suppose to protect them from a wicked world of sin? Not long. And how long my Lord must we constantly forget; oh, the blood, sweat, tears and fears of those who labored in the hot, sweltering, heated cotton fields of Alabama and the muddy tobacco fields of South Carolina that we might have a better life to live? It's not long. And then how long my Lord, and how could it be, a pure hearted man, full of the Holy Spirit, from the top of his head to the balls of his feet, wise with wisdom and knowledgeable at diction can one day take and gain the whole world in the palm of his hand;[136] snuggle it and purge it underneath the breastplate of his chest and then one day in a split second, lose all of his God-given soul[137] just for a moment of pleasure to the world? How long Lord? It's not long. Gone are the days when life was so simple then. You see the good hearted, God fearing Christian would hurry at the bedside of those who had one breath left to breathe and then pray them back to the land of the living. The preacher man and the preacher woman would stop at nothing to sup at the tables of those who had not. But, now that the last days are upon the land and of the seas, and the tempered level of mankind is at its highest peak ever; whom my Lord can I ever turn to and where, my beloved shall I ever go? Should I bend with the wind or just cast my sail, or just stay strong at the back of the rail? Should I run through the lilies, or just lie beneath the willows, or just stay strong to withstand the billows? Can I sing my song or just do a dance, or maybe thank heaven for another chance? So, whatever betides thee my love one, to me this day I say, and I say again, how long? It's not long. So, gear up thy faith with much vigor, cast thy sails against the rumbling seas, thrust thy throttle towards the heavens and soar like an eagle.[138] And if you look around one day and find me not; oh, fret not thyself, for me. For I'll be at the gates of New Jerusalem, dwelling with my Lord and Savior, Jesus, the Christ. For there's no place I'd rather be. That is the secret garden of prayer.

Just Stand

"Dedicated to Pastor & First Lady Anthony Medlock Resurrection Life Community Church of Charlotte, NC"

What good is it that a people of God can one day take and gain the whole world in the palm of their hands and then one day in a split second lose all of their God given souls just for a moment of pleasure to the world?[139]

There comes a time in everyone's life when the spirit of the living God comes beyond the midnight hour and test the very core of one's true existence. Even at a time when the world begins to cast stones and fire dots at all that you hope to be. Nevertheless, with a made up mind and a sense of urgency, there's nothing left to do, but mount up your wings like an eagle in flight,[140] for freedom is the only way out.

It is often said that good things come to those who wait upon the spirit of the Lord[141] and God helps those who help themselves, but none of these are created to be true if your soul is not anchored in His every word.

There was a time when life was so simple then. The preacher man would thirst and hunger at a chance of saving a sin sick soul. But now that the spirit of selfishness has invaded the land with so many unforgiving hearts, whom my Lord will step out and stand for the will of the kingdom?

I say and I say, again and again, ye chosen people of God, when the world begin to bury you beneath sinking sand; gear up the full armor and stand. And when the storm keeps on raging in your life and it seems like all hope is gone, just keep your eyes upon the distance shore.[142]

There's even going to come a time when you come to a cross road of a dead end situation and the spirit of the vision tears and separates the very essence of the masters plea. Oh my beloved ones to Him, JUST STAND!

Now stand when they come to and fro, when night turns to day and the season shadow its shower of blessings....STAND, and let peace be still amongst the righteous seas and let the captain of your ship navigate your every need.

Oh! Fear not thy faithful servants. Be courageous like Daniel and Noah in the days of old. He did it for them and He'll do it for you. Stand firm, faithful and true; like a rock planted by the rivers of cool and flowing waters.[143]

Stand when you are right and stand when you are wrong and stand when you are young and stand when you are old. Oh Stand! When it's cold outside even at the heat of the day, and if the winds keep blowing in your life,[144] just stand keeping your hands upon the throttle and your eyes upon the rail.
Stand and go hard after His every call, casting thy sails against unchartered waters letting fair winds and flowing seas guide you through the Kingdoms gate. For what good is it that a people of God can take and gain the whole world in the palm of their hands and then one day in a split second lose all of their God given souls just for a moment of pleasure to the world?[145]

JUST STAND!!!!!

INTERLUDE SEVEN:

Pastor Anthony Medlock

Will You Be Ready For His Return?

The Book of Revelation uncovers and concerns itself with the second coming of the Lord, Jesus Christ; and the final consummation of all things to Himself. The whole of scripture reveals to us, "Blessed is he that readeth, and they that hear the words of this prophecy, and keep those things which are written therein: For the time is at hand. (Revelation 1:3).

It's important to note the seven blessings that are bestowed upon those that not only *hear*, but also *heed*, those things which are written therein: for the time is at hand.

1. Revelation 1:3, "Blessed is he that readeth, and they that hear the words of this prophecy, and keep those things which are written therein: for the time is at hand."

2. Revelation 14:13, "And I heard a voice from heaven saying unto me, Write, Blessed are the dead which die in the Lord from henceforth: Yea, saith the Spirit, that they may rest from their labours; and their works do follow them."

3. Revelation 16:15, "Behold, I come as a thief. Blessed is he that watcheth, and keepeth his garments, lest he walk naked, and they see his shame."

4. Revelation 19:9, "And he saith unto me, Write, Blessed are they which are called unto the marriage supper of the Lamb. And he saith unto me, These are the true sayings of God."

5. Revelation 20:6, "Blessed and holy is he that hath part in the first resurrection: on such the second death hath

no power, but they shall be priests of God and of Christ, and shall reign with him a thousand years."

6. Revelation 22:7, "Behold, I come quickly: blessed is he that keepeth the sayings of the prophecy of this book."

7. Revelation 22:14, "Blessed are they that do his commandments, that they may have right to the tree of life and may enter in through the gates into the city."

Therefore, those who dismiss or denounce the truth of this prophecy, declare upon themselves the devastating wrath to come. The scriptures repeatedly summons the church and every believer not to compromise its standards, and holistic stewardship, seeing that the Lord is soon to come.

What we must understand is, that God's timetable has already been set; His clock and calendar dates are different from ours. 2 Peter 3:8-9 remind us, "But, beloved, be not ignorant of this one thing, that one day is with the Lord as a thousand years, and a thousand years as one day. The Lord is not slack concerning His promise, as some men count slackness; but is long-suffering to us-ward, not willing that any should perish, but that all should come to repentance."

The truth about the truth is, time has only been about two days, since this revelation was revealed. A question that demands an answer is, Will you be ready, for His return? *If you're not ready*, my prayer is that you urgently and sincerely repent from your sins and daily seek to have a real relationship with Jesus Christ. Psalm 86:5 "For thou, Lord art good, and ready to forgive: and plenteous in mercy unto all them that call upon thee."

Let me testify.

For our God is mighty to save and set you free! Hallelujah!!! *If you are rapture ready*, then in doing so, it becomes our responsibility to encourage others to be ready for His return. "Not forsaking the assembling of ourselves together, as the manner of some is; but exhorting one another; and so much the more, as ye see the day approaching." Hebrews 10:25 Heaven is my favorite place, where I will forever be with the Lord. What about you?

Awaiting His Return,
Minister Anthony Medlock, Pastor

CHAPTER EIGHT

Louise Tyler

About Me: Louise Tyler

- Favorite Scripture: Matthew 11:28-30

   Come unto me, all ye that labour and are heavy laden, and I will give you rest. Take my yoke upon you, and learn of me; for I am meek and lowly in heart: and ye shall find rest unto your souls. For my yoke is easy, and my burden is light.

- Pet Peeves:

   1. Slow drivers in the fast lane
   2. Liars (just be honest and I can deal with you better)
   3. Negativity/Complainers (there is good in everything and everybody)

- Favorite Foods:

   1. Sweets (homemade pound cakes/milk chocolate with almonds/pecans)
   2. Macaroni & Cheese

- Skills/Talents: (You would be surprised to know I like)

   1. Event Planning
   2. Arts & Crafts (Greeting Cards)
   3. Short Story Writer
   4. Cake Baking/Cooking

- Hobbies:

   1. Reading
   2. Traveling – Venturing Out to Places I've never been
   3. Watching Old Movies/HGTV/Hallmark & Westerns

4. Entertaining/Networking with family and friends

- Favorite Vacation Place

    1. South Africa (You have to visit here)
    2. Hawaii

A Broken Vessel, In the Master's Hands

God knew you before you were ever formed.[146]
Heartache, disappointments, loss, none of this is a surprise to Him, it's the norm.
God said in the world you will have trials and tribulations, but be of good cheer.[147]
So, no matter what the situation looks like, don't you fear.

Divorce, a broken vessel; yet you're never alone.
God will redeem the time and give you a new song.
Failing health, a broken vessel; yet by His stripes you are healed.[148]
Learn to praise God in everything, no matter how you feel.

Unemployment, a broken vessel; yet God supplies all of your needs.[149]
Trust in Him at all times,[150] and it is your soul that He will feed.
Financial woes, a broken vessel; yet if you tithe, God will pour you out a blessing.[151]
Try Him, I assure you, you will no longer be stressing.

Conviction, a broken vessel; yet, you have another chance, so don't feel down.
I've witnessed when you put it in the Master's Hands, you will rebound.
Death, a broken vessel, yet to be absent from the body, is to be present with the Lord.[152]
Think about it, they're at the Master's table, oh what a reward?

So, all I'm trying to say to you is that we're all broken vessels in the Master's hand.
He has created you specifically for His purpose and His plan.[153]

So, for every not you, for every bill that's due. For every subtraction and every distraction.
For every cry and every lie.
For every devil and every time, they said never.
For every unfilled dream and every time, you didn't make the team.
For every time you had to fret, for every not yet.
For every loss,
Just remember, God paid it all at the cross.

A Broken Vessel, In the Master's Hands

A Conversation To God

God, here I am a living testimony waiting to be told.
It's because You saw something great in me, You saved my soul.
The world has so much to offer, but it is because of You I live.
It is now that I know, that I have a purpose to fulfill.

Yesterday is gone and today I'm moving full speed ahead.
I thank you for standing in the gap when others counted me as dead.
A wretch I was, but a child of yours, now I stand.
It is with faith and prayer all things are possible, I now know that I can.

The Washington Post can't tell my story;
Because they weren't there when You revealed Yourself in Your glory.
Yes, in the past, I was ashame, but today, my life is an open book.
You paid the price a long time ago; You reached into the pit of hell, releasing me from Satan's hook.

Although for me, The Walk of Fame has no star for my name.
But when You touched me, I knew my life was no longer the same.
ABC, CBS, Fox nor CNN can share with others what You have done for me.
You have blessed me over and over with additional blessings stored up that my natural eye can't see.

A defeated foe I was, but You kept revealing Yourself more to me each day.
You have a path laid out for me and I'm not letting nothing stand in my way.
For so many years I took life for granted and didn't believe heaven or hell was real.

You have already told me you'll never leave me,[154] so I will continue to praise You no matter how I feel.

Yes, there is an economic meltdown, but I am a child of the King, so I will not fear.
The bible says, I will have some trials and tribulations, but be of good cheer.[155]
No matter what comes my way as I prepare to close out 2010, I know I have already won.
What a gift, you gave me when You gave Your one and only Son?[156]

So I can tell others to hold on, there time is coming, because You are the solid rock.
I will always remember in the book of Matthew You said to ask, seek and knock.[157]
I may not dot every I and cross every T, but I will continue to aim at the mark.
I am glad that you are not like man, You look at the heart.

I will never try to change Your word to justify my sin.
You have given me the playbook; I will live by the commandments, one through ten.[158]
So, as I now bring our conversation to an end, it is Your word that I can take to the bank.
I will honor you always with a word of thanks.

Addiction

A D D I C T I O N is a sin.
It's a battle you constantly fight, but you just can't seem to win.
First it starts so simple, yet it knows just what you like.
An addiction it is, because if feeds your appetite.

Private, yet it causes hurt and shame.
Not sure how it started, but because of it, you're no longer the same.
Lost and broken at times because of its hold.
This addiction has you and has gripped your very soul.

Yes, you can function, yet others will never know the depth.
You want to release the addiction, but it's been privately kept.
An addiction it is, and it appears out of nowhere.
You know that you're not the only one, but you wonder if anyone even cares.

For so long this addiction has had you and you don't know how to let it go.
For some it may be easy, but for you, you just don't know.
You've prayed and did without, but before you knew it, it was just a matter of time.
If you don't get a grip on your addiction, you could lose your mind.

For some, yours could be alcohol and others it could be drugs.
For some, it could be a man or a woman providing you with temporary love.
On the other hand, someone else could be wrestling with sex.
Only to leave you wondering what disease you'll have next.

Although your addiction seems innocent, ultimately it can lead to your death.

All because you can't cope with reality you tend to lose yourself.
Yes, others may attempt to prejudge you while trying to determine what you're all about.
But instead, we should pray that the Lord Almighty
bring you out.

Your private addiction is not just for you as someone else is
waiting for you to set them free.
Your addiction is waiting to leave, but you have to open up your
eyes to see.
A living testimony you are, because God Himself is the only one
who can bring you through.
Choose today to free yourself and bid your Addiction, adieu.

A Mother's Plea

I can't rest in bed, so I jump to my feet.
I realize that my child is not at home, but somewhere out in the street.
I've searched the house, called the cell phone and nothing; so, I'm up pacing the floor.
All of a sudden, I hear a noise, so I go running to see if that's my child coming through the door.

He's been distant, as our relationship has been strained for a while.
Unfortunately, as a family, communication has never been a part of our lifestyle.
I'm trying my best by keeping a roof over our head and working two jobs just to provide.
Lord, where is his father to lead, protect and guide?

Every time I turn around, he's with this girl and that girl and I often wonder what girl is next?
It's sad as a parent, I'm afraid to talk to my own child about sex.
He doesn't have a job, but every time I turn around, he has all of the latest fads.
Oh, how many times has he reminded me that he has a father that he wishes he never had?

As a mother, hearing this, what does that say about me and the man that I chose?
Your guess is as good as mine, because back then and even now, who knows?
Many times, he's in his own world and when he's home, I find him isolated in his room.
When our paths do cross, I can see in his eyes the pain and gloom.

For so long, I made an attempt to reach out, but I just didn't know how.
Wait a minute, this is my flesh and blood, I can't wait another minute, I have to do something now.
So many years I carried the weight of brokenness, guilt and shame because I had a child so young.
An epiphany hit me, God doesn't make any mistakes,[159] this is my son.

So, I must take my rightful place and be willing to put in the time.
My son will not be on the local news or the front page, for committing a crime.
We will now sit at the table and have family dinner together.
I am willing to make the necessary sacrifices for our home to be better.

Eagerly we look forward to family time and now my son is ecstatic about his education.
No more sagging pants and numerous girls as he has a new outlook on life, what a revelation?
I now plead the blood of Jesus over my son, each and every day.
Daily, we now sit down as a family to pray.

My advice to you is, "don't ever give up on your child no matter what they do."
Everything that they are and will ever accomplish all starts with you.

Beautiful Black Woman

God cared enough to have her as a part of His plan.
She is so special He created her from the rib of a man.[160]
Vulnerable at times, yet strong and solid; she bears the burdens of the weak.
No matter the struggle, she always lands on her feet.

Provider, Protector, Physician,
Teacher, Trainer, Technician, Caregiver, Coach, Counselor,
Matriarch, Maid, Mother, Father
She is Your Front, Your Back, Your Middle and everything else in between.
Of all things, she's a beautiful black queen.

She comes in every shade from mocha, dark chocolate, caramel, brown skin, light skin, dark skin and even jet black.
To provide for her family, she will work two jobs just to take up the slack.

If necessary, she will raise her family alone.
She will go the distance to take care of her home.
She's a woman of history and mystery who should be recognized each and every day.
She knows where her help comes from, so she isn't ashame to pray.

She has beauty that radiates when she walks into a room.
She handles her business at home and in the corporate boardroom.
There is something about her that make men turn their head just to take a second look.
She knows how to take something from nothing and make a meal that's off the hook.

She comes as a coke bottle, and hourglass in apple bottoms of every size.
She is amazing; you can see it in her beautiful brown eyes.
Smooth and sexy she is as you can see it in her walk.
Bold, brazing and confident is what she is, just listen to her when she talks.

So, who is this beautiful black woman?
She's You.
So, the next time you see a sister, Encourage her because she's one too.

So, beautiful, black woman I applaud you, you deserve a hand.
You have purpose and destiny in you, as God has you in His hand.

Don't Be Fooled

Shaped by the master's hand;
It is my life He has already planned.[161]
He knew me before my birth.[162]
Society can't dictate to me, my worth.
My tattoos, they don't define me.
So, don't judge me by the image that you see.
Potential dwells in me, that's why He went to Calvary.
Peer pressure is often the order of my day.
Instead of condemning me, just pray.
It's not in my cornrows, locks or the twists.
God is with me, He's always in my midst.
It's not even in the color or style of my hair.
Privately, it's God who I spend time with, in prayer.
The local news can't tell my story.
The challenges I have, is to His glory.
My bitterness is temporary as I am confused;
But I know that I am a vessel that God can use.
You question my sexuality, as if it determines my fate.
God has said, He will make the crooked things straight.[163]
No person or force can say to me, you're not the one.
I am one of God's chosen, so this can't be undone.
Clothed in wisdom all around,
Your opinions of me, no longer have me bound.
It's not in the sway of my hips.
Christ is what you hear coming from my lips.
It's not in the swag of my walk; Nor the slang when I talk.
It's not in my use of ebonics, nor the essence of my speech.
Destiny covers me from my head to my feet.
It's not in my weight or the circumference of my body size.
I am a child of the King, I'm already a God given prize.
Dark chocolate, mocha or caramel is only a pigment of the color
of my skin.
Purpose and Destiny surrounds me, so I win.

Covered in His blood and tried by the fire;
Wisdom resides within me and that's my heart's desire.
My address is noted as one that is in the hood.
Righteousness overtakes me, so don't lose sight and let that be misunderstood.
My appearance is often stereotyped because of the way I dress.
Just know that Christ is the head of my life, I am already blessed.

He Is

He is the beginning and the end.[164]
There is no in between.
He is Alpha and Omega.[165]
He is more than willing and able.
He is the rock.
All you have to do is ask, seek and knock.[166]
He is a healer.
Ask my nephew, He's a deliverer.
He is everything that you need.
It is your soul that He feeds.
He is a mystery.
All you have to do is check His history.
He can't be explained.
There is power in His name.
It is His son that He gave.[167]
It is you that He came to save.
When the trials of life won't cease;
He is the one who brings you peace.
When others rise up against you and become hostile.
He shows up and does the impossible.
When you're ready to give up, He shows up right on time.
He does things that blows the human mind.
He is and will always be.
He does things that the natural eye can't see.
Before your existence, it is your life He had already planned.
He controls life and death in the palm of His hands.[168]
He speaks and the wind obeys.
He is never too busy to listen to what you have to say.
Accept Him as Lord and Savior and He will willingly take you in.
He is the only One who can wash away your sins.[169]
So, who is He?
He's your joy from morning to night.
He makes sure that everything is alright.

When my family situation appeared full of gloom;
He took the time to show up in the court room.
When things in your life go from bad to worse;
You should be reminded that Christ hung on the cross and said,
"I Thirst."[170]
He protects you as you travel through life from day to day.
Heaven should be your home; He's already paved the way.
The Father, The Son and The Holy Ghost are one.[171]
Because He Is; you have already won.

I Pray

I pray for every person who has lost his or her way.
Please know that God can use you, He already knows about your life's resume.
I pray for every person who feels that they don't deserve another chance.
Anchor yourself in the word of God and He will help you to advance.

I pray for every person who walks around with life's extra baggage.
Trust in God, He can even reconcile your troubled marriage.
I pray for every person who didn't exercise their right to vote.
No matter your struggles, in God there is always hope.

I pray for every person who suffers from any form of addiction. God has already told you, "it's for a moment, it's a light affliction."[172]
I pray for every person that suffers from any form of abuse.
God wants you to know that He created you, you are valuable, and you are of great use.

I pray for every person who interacts with the Department of Corrections.
Jesus Christ has gone through it all and in Him there is no imperfection.
I pray for every person who suffers from any form of mental illness.
God has done some amazing things for you; don't be ashame, stand up and be a witness.

I pray for every person who suffers from any form of lack.
Always remember, man may walk away, but God always has your back.

I pray for every person who has to be mother, father, caregiver and everything else in between.
Stay focused and don't give up, God has some blessings for you that are unseen.

I pray for every person who feels their prayers are unanswered and question why the wait.
All God requires of you is to have that mustard seed faith.[173]
I pray for every person who is lonely and those with low self-esteem.
God may not come as you expect, sometimes He reveals Himself in a dream.

I pray for every person who struggle to maintain, yet, is always broke.
There is nothing too big nor impossible for God,[174] He can break every yoke.[175]
There is none like Him, He is Christ The Lord.
Um, if you could only see the things that He has in store, for the saints of New Home Baptist Church, if we all get on one accord.

I Pray, You Pray, Let's All Pray

I Pray – Part II

Lord, here I am again before you as I began to pray.
Oh heavenly Father, I ask you to hear my cry, without delay.
We are walking around not realizing that You will come like a thief in the night.[176]
Lord, it's my prayer, that we accept You as our Lord and Savior and get our souls right.

I pray for Eli, a stranger who cried before me because he was really broken by the challenges of life.
I thank You for allowing our paths to cross so that I could tell him about You, Jesus Christ.
I pray for every person who suffers from lack and truly has a genuine need.
Please help us to realize that it's mandatory; it is our soul we must daily feed.

I pray for those who wrestle in silence with their own private sins.
Please know that with God, you can overcome anything; He's just waiting for you to personally invite Him in.
I pray for those who are ashame to praise God, because they are not in rhythm or a little off beat.
Only you know what God has done for you, so stand up on your feet.

I pray for those who have lost loved ones, but I encourage you to cherish the memories to help you make it through.
One day we will be together again, but the choice is totally up to you.
I pray for every person who is still holding on to past hurt, bitterness and deep-rooted pain.
God can restore every injustice, just try calling on His name.

I pray for those who are wandering around and are truly lost.
It is for you personally, that God went to the cross.

I pray for every person who struggle with their failures and have had doors closed in their face.
Right where you are, God is still extending His mercy and His grace.

I pray for those who feel that they can't make it because of favoritism, nepotism and the world's system.
Um, if the real saints of God stood up for righteousness, what an impact we would make as Christians?
I pray for every person who battle with addictions, whether unintentional or by your own choice.
God is trying to get your attention; you may need to lay aside social media and the electronic gadgets, because sometimes God speaks in a still, quiet voice.

I pray for the homeless all over the world, even right here in the nation's Capital, Washington, DC.
Lord, I beseech you to release them from life's bondage, and hear their every plea.
I pray for the ones who must be mother, father and caregiver while always trying to hold it all together.
Beloved, trust me, with God on your side, things will get better.

I pray for the one who has received some disturbing news or an unfavorable report.
I am a living witness; God will meet you right in the midst of your current situation; for my family it was in court.
Let me be transparent for a moment, the odds were seventeen to one.
When God stamps His approval on it, no human or any other force can change what God has already done.

So, I say to every one of you, seek God daily and know that prayer is the key.
One day, He's coming back, so the question is, where will you spend eternity?

If I Had to Tell You About Christ

He is the beginning and the end and there is no in between.
He's done some miraculous things for us and many of our blessings remain to be seen.
He created the heaven and the earth and brought Adam on the scene.
It's for you and me that He died and now we can be redeemed.

He traveled the world on a mission, opening blind eyes and healing the sick.
So, don't be so quick to throw in the white towel of surrender, fight on, and don't you quit.
No matter what sins we commit, His love is unconditional, and He always provide.
When we're ready to give up, He whispers to us, "I'm right here by your side".

He fed over 5,000 with two fish and five loaves of bread.[177]
Spend some time on your own with God and stop living off what grand momma and them said.
He raised Lazarus from the dead;[178] He walked on water[179] and even turned water into wine.[180]
How many more excuses are we going to make instead of giving Him a small portion of our time?

He was beaten, spat on[181] pierced in His side and nailed to the cross.[182]
It's for you and me that He came to save, because He already knew we would be lost.
He cast out demons,[183] made a donkey to speak[184] and forgave the woman at the well.[185]

As born again, Holy Ghost filled Christians, it is Christ we must live and never be ashamed to tell.

He's the one who knows how many strands of hair we have on our head[186] and our every thought.
Satan has no control over us because it's with God's bloodstain we have been bought.
Jonah was in the belly of the whale for three days and nights and then vomited out onto dry land.[187]
We keep trying to figure things out when God has our life already planned.

He is the lily of the valley[188] and the bright morning star.[189]
No matter the road we've traveled, God will come and see about us, right where we are.
He's coming back one day and according to His word no one knows the day or the hour.[190]
What are we waiting for, choose ye this day to accept Him and experience His awesome power?

Life's Verses

You see in John 16:33 God said, "You will have trials and
tribulations."[191]
But I want you to know that your current state is not your final
destination.
Every argument, struggle and battle is not designed for
you to fight.
In Matthew 11:30, God said, "For my yoke is easy and my
burden is light."[192]

Don't focus on whether or not you measure up to society's
standards.
God has already given you the playbook in Exodus 20, read His
Ten Commandments.[193]
Life is a rollercoaster and through it all, you must learn to stand.
In Jeremiah 29:11, it's you He had in mind and He's already laid
out your plan.[194]

Just for a moment; put your mind on rewind, it's in John 3:16,
"God gave His only begotten son."[195]
So, for every demon and every setback that comes your way,
know that you've already won.
You see, God is so big, and our minds can't always comprehend
the reasons.
It's in Ecclesiastes 3:1, He's already told us, "It's a time and
a season."[196]

You see that diagnosis, or bad news you have received, I
encourage you to seek God and pray.
Spend a little time checking out that Hebrews 11 faith.[197]
I understand that you've been through the storm and rain, but we
all have a story that need to be told.
I just want you to know that it's in Psalm 23 that He will restore
your soul.[198]

He's Alpha and Omega[199] from Genesis to Revelation.
No matter what comes your way, never lose hope, always have some expectations.
I'm not telling you what I've heard, nor seen, but it's what I know.
Develop a relationship with Him and take Him wherever you go.

THE CRACK

It's small, a glitch, but yet it carries so much weight.
Often, it's insignificant, but sometimes it determines our fate.
For example, it's like a tire with a slow leak.
Today we are standing, but tomorrow that one setback, knocks us off our feet.

You see, every one of us has experienced a crack in our life.
It comes in many forms; such as pain, bitterness, unforgiveness and strife.
For you, it may be a battle that you wrestle with as a stronghold.
Take a moment to read from Genesis to Revelation to see how the stories unfold.

We lose focus as our attention is geared towards that small crack.
Just think for a minute, God has blessed us over and over; He has our back.
For you, that crack is that thing that won't release you from your past.
You act as though everything is ok, but you're really hiding behind a mask.

You see that crack holds us hostage to a particular situation.
God wants us to get up from where we are, with no hesitation.
For you, that crack comes from nowhere and you find yourself off balance.
Sometimes it's God's way of getting our attention; He has to put us in complete silence.

Have you ever had a crack in your life, you know that thing that just won't let you go?
Well God said, "I will never leave nor forsake you"[200] and that's one thing that you should know.

A crack is not always bad, as God specializes in our brokenness, guilt and shame.
He loves and cares for us, try calling on His name.

For some of you, that crack consumes you and controls your mind.
God wants you to know that He forgives you and its some things, you must leave behind.
That crack is nothing but satan, who wants you to have a pity party and remain in your sin.
God has outstretched hands to you, because it's your soul He wants to mend.

That crack is that thing that eats away at your spirit only to annoy.
God wants you to have peace, and He will restore your joy.
For some of you, that crack has attacked your finances, your marriage, your children, your home and has altered your behavior.
I want you to know that there is no issue that is too big, nor impossible for God as He is our Lord and Savior.

As it has been said before, "trouble don't last always."
It's time for us to get busy living and give God all the praise.

The Generation

You're brought into this world and no one knows what you will become.
You want the best life has to offer, and then some.
Growing up where love was absent, and chaos was the order of the day.
You're your own man; you don't care what anyone has to say.

It's so easy for you to get your hands on the weapon of your choice.
As you pull the trigger, you can hear momma's voice.
You feel that there is no destiny or purpose on your life, so here you are out on the street.
Satan took control a long time ago, as you so easily gave into defeat.

An education is something that you lack, because you just can't comprehend.
You're tired of living this life of committing sin after sin.
The jails and prisons are filled with your young black brothers.
Your beautiful black Queen can't find her King because so many of you are undercover.

The cemetery awaits to greet another family that is overwhelmed with grief.
Man, if you would only walk the other way, "ah what a relief"?
Broken, lost and confused only leads you to suffer with so much pain and strife.
You only act out because you have no one to guide you on this journey called life.

A life is allegedly taken over a pair of tennis shoes.
It's your spirit that will not let you rest, and it's your soul that you ultimately lose.

It's nothing for you to concoct the plan to commit your
next crime.
Prison awaits you, as you return to do more time.

Working a nine to five and making honest money is not in
your profile;
But wearing your pants sagging and a body covered with tattoos
is your style.
Reading the newspaper and watching the news, you might just be
the highlight of the day.
You will be the discussion in households, but does anyone
think to pray?

I can't leave you here as your future is in your hands; so, I'll ask,
what are you going to do?
You're valuable, shed your old habits and seek Christ, who died
just for YOU.
God is a loving God, and He will give you chance after chance.
Love, redemption and purpose will overtake you, if you're willing
to advance.

The Inner Man's Struggle

I am eternally grateful to live, breathe and abide on this earth.
Although there are times when I reflect over my life, I question my birth.
You see, I know that the world owes me nothing, yet I seem to always be bound.
No matter which way I turn, I feel alone, frustrated, misunderstood, rejected and always down.

I know that my family loves me, but affection is rarely something that is expressed.
Too often I am stereotyped because I don't measure up to society's view of success.
Yeah, I know I must obtain an education or some type of trade just to survive.
How can I admit my faults and failures, when I have so much pride?

I look at others and they appear to always be one step ahead.
I know I've done some stupid things, and it's by the grace of God that I'm not dead.
You see as a man; I have some faults and issues that I just can't admit.
There are times that I know my family is ready to give up on me, but I just can't quit.

Too often I observe as people watch me and attempt to size me up.
There are times that I cry myself to sleep, longing for my mother's touch.
My dad walked out and never cared enough to pour knowledge into me to invest.
Oh, how many times have I heard, "you'll never amount to anything" but hey, I want life's best.

Growing up poor, I figured life would always be a struggle for me,
    so I never set any type of goal.
If only I had someone to pour wisdom and guidance into my
    lonely and aching soul.
You know, I felt bad always holding my hand out waiting for
    someone to provide me with relief.
It was too often people sat and conversated with me, never realizing I was suffering silently in grief.

No longer will I be held captive by the pressures of life or be held
    down by any type of chain.
I know that I better get moving or else life will remain the same.
So many times, I blamed society for not offering me the opportunity to take that chance.
But then I realized it was up to me, to make the appropriate
    choices in life, if I wanted to advance.

Mothers have been there right from the start, but can't always
    provide us with that helping hand.
We must appreciate our sisters for standing and guiding us along
    this journey in becoming a man.
So, I apologize to all the women I took advantage of, because if
    they only knew, I was really lost.
But today, I can stand and say that I thank God for going to
    the cross.

So, to all of you men out there, it's okay to cry and even make
    some mistakes, but don't stay there.
Trust in our Lord Jesus Christ and take it to Him in prayer.
All of your problems will not disappear, so don't you dare give
    into defeat.
I guarantee you if you take your burdens to the Lord, He's the
    best person you'll ever meet.

Thank You Lord

As we travel daily on Life's Expressway, your protecting power is indeed a privilege.
Thank you Lord, for thinking enough of us and creating us in your own image.
While on this journey, we cross over Trials and Tribulations Avenue.
Thank you Lord, because it's your grace and mercy that gets us through.

There have been some ups and downs as we stopped by Low Self Esteem and Depression Lane.
Thank you Lord that you didn't leave us where we were and we were able to call on your name.
In route, we find ourselves sitting at Unforgiveness and Bitterness Alley.
Thank you Lord for reaching down and pulling us from the lowest valley.

Hurt, despair, loneliness, they all lead us to a dead-end street.
Thank you Lord, for giving us another chance by not allowing us to suffer in defeat.
Drugs, alcohol and various addictions drove us up Hallucination Hill.
Thank you Lord for saving us and allowing us to be a part of your will.

Living on Memory Lane, we wallowed in sin and did every unthinkable deed.
Thank you Lord, for sending and angel along the way who met us at our very need.
As we find ourselves on Around The Way Circle, we are constantly in a fight.

Thank you Lord for putting us in a deep sleep and showing us your guiding light.

Lord, we haven't dotted every I and we haven't crossed every T.
Thank you Lord for sending Your son, to save someone like me.
As we take the interstate of No Matter The Multitudes Of Our Many Sins;
Thank You Lord, because You have been right there with us to the very end.

We camped out on We Had Our Share Of Problems Boulevard and it wasn't enough to take us out.
Thank you Lord, for sending a Savior to show us what Christ is all about.
As we exit the ramp For Every Setback That We Thought Was A Delay;
Thank you Lord, for humbling us and teaching us that we always need to pray.

As we sit here at the intersection of How Am I Going To Make It, we ponder if this is all by happenstance?
Thank you Lord, for every road that we've traveled, because You still give us chance after chance.
As we traveled down the highway of How Long Lord, with our minds totally In A Daze;
Thank you Lord that we still have breath, and we owe You all of the praise.

So, Lord;
For every tear,
for every not yet,
for every hurt,
for every pain,
for every trial,
for every ache,

for every no,
for every not you,
for every unseen danger,
for every broken promise,
for every lost loved one,
for every time they walked out,
for every time they didn't come home,
for every rejection,
for every disappointment,
for every insult,
for every failure,
for every if I knew then, what I know now,
for every cry,
You saw much further ahead then what I could ever see.

Thank You Lord, Thank You Lord, Thank You Lord;
For You alone, know what's best for me.

When God Doesn't Make Sense

Whether Harvard, Yale, Princeton or your pedigree of education.
The "bible" is God's word that is so full of information.
It's great when you read or hear of the stories of old.
For you and me, God performed miracles and today they're still being told.

No matter what you're going through, don't lose sight by having a bitter attitude.
Just remember God took two fish and five loaves and fed the multitude.[201]
For every direction you turn, there is a roadblock and you can't move ahead.
You know God is in the blessing business, after four days He raised Lazarus from the dead.[202]

When you're a soldier for Christ, let others know that God will remove all pain, bitterness and strife.
Tell them if they don't believe you, they can look back over your life.
Rejection, imperfection and always in the way of correction, you feel like you've never won.
Only the Lord God Almighty can have a 90-year-old woman to bear a son.[203]

So, for every denial, and every no that is in your life, it's only because it's not the appointed time.
You know the Great "I Am"[204] walks on water and even turns water into wine."[205]
Okay, I understand that you don't have what you want, but Jehovah-Raah supplies all of your needs.[206]
Because you're His child, He will go above and beyond, just to bless your very seed.

So, there's no need to make things complex, become upset, distressed or depressed.
Because if you don't receive anything else, you're already blessed.

You can't wrap your mind around the chaos going on in your life, so you ask God, "what is this all about?"
Let me remind you God spoke to the fish, and by His word, the fish spit Jonah out.[207]
You're suffering from the loss of a love one, or you may have pain in your body, and so no one understands how you really feel.
I suggest you trust Jehovah Rapha, He's the Lord who heals.[208]

Bills are due, the children are not in line, and the job is getting on your nerves; so, what a colossal?
Beloved, just know that with God, all things are possible.[209]
You went left, when God told you to go right, so by all accounts you could be dead;
But our God loads us daily with benefits and provides us with our daily bread.[210]

He divided the Red Sea.[211]
I don't know about you, but that's a miracle to me.
He had ravens to bring Elijah something to eat.[212]
Only our Lord and Savior, can make a donkey to speak.[213]
He speaks to the wind and at His word, it obeys.[214]
He's been too good; you owe Him all the praise.

So, I don't know what has happened in your life where you ponder, "God this doesn't make sense."
I'm a living witness that in the court room, Jehovah Shammah was our best defense.

New Home Baptist Church Poetic Voices Ministry

You Don't Understand

Take a moment to reflect on your life, and you will wonder where the time has gone.
You haven't achieved the lifestyle that you want, so you now question yourself, "where did I go wrong"?
Life, only a four-letter word, yet it's full of ever-changing events.
One minute you're smiling and the next minute you're angry and ready to vent.

You encounter a number of people every day, some with smiles and some with frowns.
Don't allow life circumstances dictate to you, whether you're going to be up or down.
You think that you're the only one hurting and no one seems to understand.
Haven't you realized by now that God created you and He has you in His plan?

You don't understand, I'm lonely and I'm tired of being alone.
Have you humbled yourself before God, don't forget He's always on the throne?
You don't understand, I don't know how I'm going to pay my bills.
Don't you know that you serve a mighty God, and we're all a part of His will?

You don't understand, I don't know where I'm going to lay my head tonight.
My, my, my, learn to focus on God, and He will guide you both day and night.
You don't understand, it's a struggle for me to live one day at a time.
Don't you know that God is awesome? Look at His marvelous works, He's forever showing you a sign.

You don't understand, my children are either in jail or acting crazy.
Well, you can continue to have a pity party, or learn to praise God and stop being lazy.
You don't understand, I'm doing drugs, drinking alcohol and fornicating while walking around in a daze.
Don't you know that God wants you to turn your life around and give Him all the praise?

You don't understand, I don't know when I will receive my next meal.
Have you honestly sought God, because He's still real?
You don't understand, I have been physically beaten and robbed of my self-esteem.
Don't you know that you should always pray, no matter how bad things seem?

You don't understand, I don't' have a job and I don't know how I'm going to make ends meet.
Stop blaming everybody else for your downfalls and learn to stand on your own two feet.
You don't understand, I don't have a car and I'm always broke.
Don't you know that God has already orchestrated your day, before you even woke?

You don't understand, it's hard for me to deal with my mother's, son's, daughter's death and I feel so lost.
Beloved, God already knew of these things, yet He still hung out on the cross.
If there is a God, why is there so much killing, sickness, suffering, pain and strife?
Just know that God never promised you a world without trials or tribulations during this journey called life.

You don't understand, my life is full of heartache and pain.

Always remember God has never promised you a life full of sunshine, without some rain.
Please understand that God loves you in spite of where you've been and the road you've traveled thus far.
Learn to trust Him, and He will accept you right where you are.

INTERLUDE EIGHT:

Reverend Ronald K. Miner, Pastor

1. *What are your thoughts about the younger generation, and how they can get focused on being kingdom ready to make it into heaven?*

RM The young people won't be focused until adults get focused. They can't raise themselves, so they need examples and to be taught how to live kingdom lifestyles. In these days there is a lack of kingdom examples.

2. *Why do you think so many are falling away from the faith?*

RM Because the bible says so. Most people normally read the bible on Sundays. But you have to have a daily devotion with Christ by reading His word, to keep you covered. Plus, you don't know what you're going to encounter in your everyday life and there are false teachers out there. If you don't know what the word says yourself, you won't be able to rightly divide the word of truth for yourself.[215]

3. *Why do you think homosexuality and lesbianism is tolerated and accepted in society today?*

RM We can convince ourselves to believe anything is right. But the way to come back to truth is through the word, and the word says homosexuality is an abomination.[216] God loves us all, but He doesn't love what we do. God does not want us to bash homosexuals. He wants us to share the word with them. You have to be surgically minded when handling folks so that we cut the sin without cutting the sinner.

4. *Let's talk about Paul a little bit. Paul was a well-known sinner. What are your thoughts about Paul and his life?*

RM Paul once said that he was the "Chief of Sinners."[217] The only reason Paul was able to say that was because he hadn't met Ron Miner yet! *chuckles*. Seriously though, God tolerated Paul because He chose to use Paul to be the author of two thirds of the New Testament. "Christ died so that we would escape the penalty of sin, which is death."[218] The bible still says that "we will reap what we sow."[219] He didn't die so we would escape the punishment.

    5. *Switching gears. Temptation is something. Why do you think it's so challenging to overcome?*

RM I am a single Pastor. For seventeen years, I was married and never slept with anyone else. Over the last year when it ended, I wanted to tell God "I don't want to do this anymore." People often come to me and tell me at the end of the service, how blessed they were by my sermon. But, where is my peace? God, I did what You told me to do for them, but who do I talk to? That's when God said, "my strength is made perfect in your weakness."[220] Being strong, is knowing where you're weak. Know your weakness and stay away from it.

    6. *People say that the anti-christ is coming soon. What are your thoughts on that?*

RM There is always a mess before the miracle, but you never should miss the message. There's mess we are living in and seeing right now. The miracle will take place when Christ comes, and He's soon to do that, but the message is we should pay attention to what's going on. The bible tells us what will take place, which is what's happening right now. Satan is using so many different people to do his work. That's why churches are losing members. The bible tells Christians "not to be anxious for anything."[221] But the devil is very anxious because he knows he has a short amount of time left to get as many people as he can. He wants to confuse folks. 2 Timothy 3:5 lets us know that people will have a "form of godliness, but deny the power thereof." Satan can quote more scriptures than any one of us, but he'll never be able to live it. People will speak to you in foreign tongues and curse you out in English. Their walk should match their witness–always.

You know, we fell three ways. Meaning, the devil used a woman, a man and a tree to get us to sin in the Garden of Eden. God told man, "have whatever you like but don't bother the tree of life."[222] We didn't listen, therefore, we fell. To fix us back up and reconcile us back to the Father, God used the same thing. A man, a woman and a tree. He used Mary as the woman. He used Jesus as the man, and Calvary as the tree; and He fixed us right back up again.

7. *In three words, what do YOU think heaven is like?*

RM Heaven is like where there is no more pain or suffering. However, heaven is a holding cell. When people die, they either go to heaven or hell. They both are a holding cell. It's not where we'll spend eternity. We are going to spend eternity in the New Jerusalem. Those that are not in Christ are going to spend eternity in the lake of fire. Just like if you get arrested in Prince George's County, you get arrested and sent to the local jail. After your trial and conviction, you're sent to prison. You don't spend life in jail, you spend life in prison. Prison is different from jail. So to answer your question directly, I believe heaven is like: "Home Sweet Home."

Endnotes

1. Ecclesiastes 3:1
2. Matthew 11:28
3. Proverbs 31:10
4. Proverbs 31:30
5. Proverbs 31:31
6. Proverbs 31:10
7. Romans 8:28
8. Proverbs 3:5
9. Psalm 139:14
10. 1 Peter 2:9
11. Romans 8:3
12. Hebrews 11:1
13. Luke 2:7
14. Acts 19:36
15. 1 Timothy 6:10
16. Revelation 13:17
17. Matthew 7:15-16, Matthew 24:4-5
18. Romans 7:21

19 2 Peter 3:9
20 Romans 8:37
21 John 3:16
22 Romans 7:15
23 1 Corinthians 12:9
24 Matthew 17:20
25 Psalm 27:14
26 Ephesians 2:8-9
27 Genesis 32:26
28 Psalm 25:4-12
29 Psalm 32:1
30 Galatians 6:7
31 Ibid
32 1 Thessalonians 5:17
33 Isaiah 42:8
34 Romans 3:23
35 Philippians 1:6
36 Proverbs 3:5-6
37 Colossians 3:23
38 Ibid
39 Mark 9:29
40 1 Thessalonians 5:7

41 Galatians 6:7

42 Matthew 5:44

43 Proverbs 22:6

44 Colossians 3:23

45 Ibid

46 2 Corinthians 5:7

47 1 John 4:4

48 Romans 4:17

49 Ibid

50 2 Corinthians 12:9

51 Psalm 42:9

52 Proverbs 3:5

53 2 Corinthians 12:9

54 2 Corinthians 4:17

55 1 Corinthians 15:57

56 Matthew 24:27

57 Romans 14:8

58 Revelations 22:17

59 Daniel 9:3

60 1 Corinthians 15:31

61 Proverbs 3:5

62 Ephesians 6:10

63 Matthew 17:20

64 Jeremiah 29:11

65 Isaiah 55:8

66 Lamentations 3:22-23

67 The Census Bureau's International Data Base – June 13, 2018 – census.gov

68 Ecclesiastes 3:1

69 Psalm 30:5

70 Galatians 5:22-23

71 1 Peter 2:9

72 Genesis 2:18

73 1 Corinthians 13:1-2

74 Genesis 2:23

75 Matthew 5:44

76 2 Timothy 2:15

77 Matthew 17:20

78 Luke 6:45

79 The Joe Madison Show/Town Hall Meeting

80 Michelle Alexander, October 12, 2011 – The Huff Post

81 Galatians 5:22-23

82 1 Thessalonians 5:17

83 Isaiah 54:17

84 1 Corinthians 16:13

85 1 Peter 5:6

86 John 14:1

87 Galatians 5:22-23

88 Isaiah 54:17

89 John 4:23

90 1 Peter 2:9

91 1 Corinthians 6:20

92 Jeremiah 29:11

93 John 3:19

94 Romans 6:16

95 Romans 6:1-3

96 1 Peter 1:16

97 Romans 12:2

98 Matthew 5:14

99 Philippians 1:6

100 2 Corinthians 4:8-9

101 2 Corinthians 12:9

102 Romans 8:38-39

103 2 Corinthians 4:17

104 Philippians 3:10

105 Isaiah 61:3

106	Matthew 17:20
107	Proverbs 3:5
108	Author Edward Mote, "My Hope is Built on Nothing Less" Hymn
109	Author William Cowper, "There Is A Fountain" Hymn
110	New Home Baptist Church Covenant, Pastor Bobby D. Hicks, Landover, MD
111	Revelation 22:13
112	Isaiah 40:31
113	Psalm 89:14
114	Romans 6:23
115	Psalm 121-4-8
116	Matthew 11:29-30
117	Author, Arthur Fletcher, Former Head of United Negro College Fund
118	Romans 8:35
119	Mark 8:36
120	John 14:1
121	John 3:16
122	Mark 16:19
123	Isaiah 58:7
124	Author Edward Mote, "My Hope is Built on Nothing Less" Hymn
125	2 Corinthians 5:8

126	John 15:13
127	Revelation 22:13
128	Matthew 22:37
129	New Home Baptist Church "Theme/Motto", Pastor Bobby D. Hicks, Landover, MD
130	John 15:13
131	The Washington Glass 1854 Hymn, "The Sinner's Cure"
132	Psalm 37:23
133	Proverbs 3:5
134	Aretha Franklin, "Walk In The Light" Lyrics
135	Matthew 24:36
136	Mark 8:36
137	Matthew 16:26
138	Psalm 37:1
139	Mark 8:36
140	Isaiah 40:31
141	Ibid
142	Author Douglas Miller, "My Soul Has Been Anchored in the Lord"
143	Psalm 1:3
144	Author Douglas Miller, "My Soul Has Been Anchored in the Lord"
145	Mark 8:36

146	Jeremiah 1:5
147	John 16:33
148	Isaiah 53:5
149	Philippians 4:19
150	Psalm 62:8
151	Malachi 3:10
152	2 Corinthians 5:8
153	Jeremiah 29:11
154	Hebrews 13:5
155	John 16:33
156	John 3:16
157	Matthew 7:7
158	Exodus 34:28
159	1 Timothy 4:4
160	Genesis 2:21-23
161	Jeremiah 29:11
162	Jeremiah 1:5
163	Isaiah 45:2
164	Revelation 1:8, 1:11, 21:6, 22:13
165	Ibid
166	Matthew 7:7
167	John 3:16

168	Deuteronomy 30:15, 19, Job 12:9-10
169	Psalm 51:2
170	John 19:28
171	1 John 5:7
172	2 Corinthians 4:17
173	Luke 17:6, Matthew 17:20
174	Luke 1:37
175	Isaiah 58:6
176	2 Peter 3:10
177	Matthew 14:17-21
178	John 11:1-44
179	Matthew 14:22-36
180	John 2:1-10
181	Matthew 26:67
182	John 19:34, Luke 23:32-33, Isaiah 53:5
183	Mark 16:17
184	Numbers 22:28
185	John 4:1-42
186	Luke 12:7
187	Jonah 1:17, Jonah 2:10
188	Solomon 2:1
189	Revelation 22:16

190	Matthew 24:36
191	John 16:33
192	Matthew 11:30
193	Exodus 20:3-17
194	Jeremiah 29:11
195	John 3:16
196	Ecclesiastes 3:1
197	Hebrews 11
198	Psalm 23:3
199	Revelation 1:8, 21:6, 22:13
200	Hebrews 13:5
201	Matthew 14:17-21
202	John 11:1-44
203	Genesis 17:16-19, 21:3
204	Genesis 17:1, Exodus 3:14, 6:2, John 6:48
205	Matthew 14:22-36, John 2:10
206	Philippians 4:19
207	Jonah 1:17, 2:10
208	Deuteronomy 32:39
209	Matthew 19:26
210	Psalm 68:19
211	Psalm, 78:13, 106:9, 136:13, Exodus 14:21

212	1 Kings 17:4-8
213	Numbers 22:28
214	Matthew 8:23-27, Mark 4:41
215	2 Timothy 2:15
216	Leviticus 18:22, Leviticus 20:13
217	1 Timothy 1:15
218	Romans 6:23
219	Galatians 6:7
220	2 Corinthians 12:9
221	Philippians 4:6
222	Genesis 2:16-17

CPSIA information can be obtained
at www.ICGtesting.com
Printed in the USA
LVHW051826200422
716610LV00010B/339